AUTHENTICALLY CELESTE

The Poetry of a Private Soul

Celeste Quackenbush

1ˢᵗ Edition 2026

ISBN Paperback: 978-1-970487-11-4
ISBN Hardcover: 978-1-970487-12-1
LCCN: 2026904467
Cover Design: Celeste Quackenbush
Printed in the United States of America

For permissions or inquiries:
ceeq2000@gmail.com

Publisher:
Bridge Publisher
www.bridgepublisher.com

I would like to dedicate this book to:
"BLINK"

Thank you, for being the dearest friend and the most support ever. Without your encouragement, this book would not have been. I am forever grateful. Again, I will always thank you.

Celeste Q.

Blink

You're just a blink on my home screen
That flashes now and then.
You're here and there and on and off
And I never know just when.

You bring with you a moment
That lightens up my day.
Just when I start to open up,
You blink and you've gone away!

I don't know where you went to,
Someplace in the vast blue net.
I don't know when or if you'll be back again.
As we've never even met.

But I find that when we've chatted
A smile lights up my face.
But then the light blinks out again
And you're off somewhere in space.

My mind says "Don't be stupid,
Stop and really think"
My inner self keeps warning me.
But my soul looks for that Blink.

Celeste Q.

Table of Contents

Blink

The Pearl--i

The Words You See --ii

Blame It On My Pen--iii

Introduction

Category 1 **Family, Friends, Frivolities**

The Dusty Road ---3

Resolution 2025 --4

Friends ---6

Vette--7

Feb 27, 1904 --8

Party Time-- 10

The Naked Poet-- 11

My Back Yard -- 12

The Hardest Choice -- 13

Today Is Fateday --- 14

My Legacy --- 15

One True Friend --- 17

I Try -- 18

Strings--- 19

Someone Special --- 20

Our Son --- 21

Bye Bye My Canadian Guy --- 22

Helpless--- 24

The Game Of Control -- 26

If Tomorrow Starts Without Me --- 27

Christmas --- 28

The Artist -- 29

My Son-- 30

My Friend The Almost Robber -- 31

Custody -- 33

Freedom-- 34

Christmas Ghost --- 35

Mom (Post Trauma)-- 36

Bubbling Brook-- 37

Shoveling Snow's Musing--- 39

Category 2   **Spiritual/Soul growth**

Oh Lord I Pray --- 43

The Price--- 44

Just The Puppet -- 45

Dreams And Wishes --- 46

Your Ghost --- 47

Through the Lens Backwards -- 49

Tired Eyes --- 51

Mother-- 52

Then I Found The Box-- 54

Earning Eternity -- 56

I've Lost My Smile -- 57

This Poet's Job -- 58

The Perfect Child-- 59

When I Was The Victim --- 60

Know Me By Name. -- 63

Remorse-- 64

The Rabbit Holes -- 65

Mellowing --- 66

Storms Of Life -- 67

A Stranger's Eyes-- 68

My Other Side --- 70

Paper Doll World-- 71

Lifelines -- 72

My Past Life --- 73

Your Wakeup Call --- 74

Chaos Conspiracies And Quests -- 75

Life in Retrospect --- 77

Nature's Co-dependency --- 78

Category 3 **True Love**

Every Night -- 83

The Pit -- 84

Love --- 86

It Just Is --- 87

My Love's Lullaby -- 88

I Love You --- 89

Always Knew -- 90

Yesterday I Cried--- 91

Why -- 92

Unconditional Love-- 93

My Cool Breeze --- 95

"One"--- 96

The Amount I Love You -- 98

Gratitude--- 99

Awakening Souls---100

One True Emotion ---102

Loneliness Of Solitude ---103

No Wishy-Washy Love --104

No Words--105

You Are My World ---106

Your Gift --107

Eternally --- 108

The Answer -- 109

Time Is Fluid -- 111

Don't -- 112

Acceptance -- 114

Don't Talk -- 115

Totality Of My Love --- 116

Chameleon--- 117

My Best Friend -- 118

Walk With Me --- 119

My Measurement Of Love --- 120

My Love --- 121

The Word Commitment -- 122

I Cherish You --- 123

Parallel Worlds --- 124

Familiar Love --- 125

I Look For You -- 126

Falling--- 127

It Is Meant To Be-- 128

Questions --- 129

Category 4 **Heartbreak**

Dear God-- 133

Dream's Bite--- 134

This Last Teardrop -- 135

Pieces of Me--- 136

Putting Back The Pieces--- 137

Doing Time-- 139

Before You -- 140

The Reality Slap -- 141

The Path-- 142

Lessons Untold -- 143

Love's Pain --- 144

The Hurt Within --- 145

Disinfecting Love --- 146

The Fool -- 147

Still I Stayed -- 148

Just Play --- 149

Broken Tea Cup -- 150

Category 5 **Depression**

I Pray -- 153

Inner Strength -- 154

When You Cry -- 155

Childhood Dreams -- 156

Depression -- 157

A Better Life --- 158

The Longest Day --- 159

Secret Strength --- 160

Resilience -- 161

Panic --- 162

Don't Want To Be -- 163

Can You Shake It? --- 164

Category 6 **Love in 5D**

Lord Of The Universe -- 167

Is it Me You're Looking For? -------------------------------------- 168

You're my Candle -- 169

Love In 5D -- 170

Online Love --- 171

The Tablet -- 172

Fading -- 173

Emoji Love Poem --- 174

Emoji Love Poem --175

New Start --176

You're There. --177

Good Morning Babygirl--178

Where? --179

Just Wishful Thinking --180

Today I Say Goodbye. --181

When The Muse Is Amused ---182

About the Author

The Pearl

The good girl or the bad?
The saucy or the sad.
The one that dresses up so fine
Or in her denims clad.

I am positive or I'm negative,
I am passive or I fight.
I'm the tough one like a marshmallow,
Doesn't matter-do it right!

I'm the listener or the yacker,
I am shy but I've been bold.
I passively fight for what is right,
I am young but I am old.

I am wise but I'm naive,
I feel intensely yet often numb.
I cry or laugh hysterically,
I am loud or I am mum.

I'm an enigma but so familiar
I'm a foe or I'm a friend.
I am happy or I'm sad
I'm a quitter to the very end.

No shades of gray, all's black or white
My mind is wrong, my heart is right.
I am well-grounded but I fly.
I am the Pearl-Gemini!

Celeste Q.

The Words You See

I do not write my poetry
My pen writes me.
I can't pick and choose the words I use
Nor the final poem you'll see.

I have no say in what to write
Nor when it comes to me.
The midnight oil many times
Has set my spirit free.

I'm the weather vein of life's torments,
Or so it seems to me.
To pen the heartaches and sorrows
And warn humanity.

The pain I write I've lived through,
The warnings - other's plight.
Our hatred for our kindred souls
Keeps me up at night.

No, I do not write my poetry.
I never have a choice.
It's all the things I see and feel
That gives my pen its voice.

Celeste Q.

Blame It On My Pen

I write of things that plant a seed.
Are mine not good enough to read?
The things that others might not see.
Not often are they reflections of me.

I write of things that come from where?
Of pain, and misery and yes, despair.
I like to keep my poems light and airy.
But my pen tears the wings off my fairy!

The pen I hold has its own mind,
It releases the word it feels at the time
Is right for growth- not right for me.
I'm just its slave mechanically.

Who said the pen sets the Poet's soul free?
No one I know - certainly not me!
It makes you reflect on your inner disdain.
Impervious to your screams of pain.

It makes you examine every small weakness,
Then sets it on paper proclaiming - it teaches?
"Teaches you what?" I asked my damn pen.
To examine your emotions again and again.

"I've been down that rabbit hole how many times?
I've written the words, compiled all the lines"
"Do it again" is the message I hear from my pen,
"Till you get it all right and just maybe then,
I'll release you to rest a short little spell.
But not for too long, you've got tales to tell."

"And make no mistake, don't throw me away.
The next pen will work you both night and day!"
So now here I sit with my paper and pen.
Wondering what I'll write next and also just when.

Celeste Q.

Introduction

This book of poetry is the author's first. It spans several decades with diverse topics in poetry. Written both from the life experiences of the author, those of others that touched in some way and some that were just meant to be written.

Category 1

**Family,
Friends,
Frivolities**

The Dusty Road

Upon this pillow I lay my head
To rest my weary soul.
Many a long road I've travelled in dread,
To this world I've given my all.

I close my eyes and drift into to sleep
To the quiet surrender of my thoughts.
And now I'm left unable to speak
Yet I know it is him whom I sought.

So, lord as I travel along my path
This dark and dusty road.
Let angels gather me within their song
As the gates of heaven open.

Give me a place where I can be
Rested and revived and renewed.
Carry my soul through eternity
This pleasure I await from you.

The gifts on this earth are very few
That the body needs to thrive.
But I took the gifts given by you
And refused to claim them as mine.

I pray to you Lord for forgiveness
For how I have wasted my days.
And now hope to be able to walk your path
And that you will guide my way.

Celeste Q.

Resolution 2025

I'm better than that I told myself
For longer than I care to remember.
I can get past all that, I kidded myself
While it still smoldered on the embers.

Yes, I was abused since childhood
Both physically and mentally.
Cursed at and strapped almost daily
By a mother with no empathy.

As I shrunk into this shell of mine
My determination kept on growing.
And as my voice grew weaker I told
Myself the hurt was never showing.

I penned my hopes, my dreams, my fears
Always in my book.
This carried me safely through the years
I tucked my torture and my tears
Safely in their nook.
Where no one else would ever look.

I'd lived through threats both gun and knife
At least eight times God saved my life.
I wrote, carried on, fooled myself I was strong
Dependent on my pen and book.
The only place that I truly belonged.

Then came the day to face true love.
The universe sent the perfect man.
One that lit my whole world up
And I realized just what and who I am.

I wasn't afraid to show my love,
And I wasn't afraid of the dance.
But came the time to meet my love?
I just couldn't take the chance.
I retreated back inside my book
Without a single glance.

Our meeting loomed so did my fright.
I clutched my book in my left so tight
And tore my heart out with my right.
While with self-worth I violently fought
My love waited there alone, for naught.

So, here's to 2025!
I pray it finds me still alive.
All the years I saved my mind
I'd left my self-esteem behind!

So this year's task has been preset
I'm not finished with me yet.
I'm working hard for just one chance
To feel truly worthy of romance.

Celeste Q.

Friends

You've passed through my life
Like a bird overhead,
So brief in flight, yet beautiful.

And I've measured my days with your memories
And my worth by your kind deeds.

I cherish each of you tho' we're apart
You are with me, a part of me.
That will always be mine.

I have loved each of you in my way
That cannot change for it has happened.

My future will be shaped
By what you've given to my past,
Thus, my life is a reflection of our friendship.

I thank God for my friends
For without you I'd be nothing.

Celeste Q.

Vette

Today I warm your hands.
I clasp them gently in mine.
The tears I hold back,
This will be the very last time.

I look into those eyes so tired
And I see all the memories we share,
And before you leave me forever
Please know just how much I care.

I'll cherish your kind gentle laughter
And the love you so freely gave.
You will stay in my heart forever.
Your friendship made me brave.

May God cradle you gently in heaven.
May you find comfort in his warm embrace.
May his angels carry you like a treasure
In awe of your humble grace.

Goodbye for now my dear friend
'Til we meet in some faraway lands.
I can't make this journey with you,
For now, I'm honored to just warm your hands.

Celeste Q.

Feb 27, 1904

Who took your life we'll never know
Time has erased all facts.
The evidence and the killer both
Have slipped between the cracks.

At seventeen your life was snubbed
Taken from you in a flash.
Leaving loved one's reeling without
Knowing who'd done the task.

Opinions flowed quite generously
Each local with their own.
The reason and the method of death
Varied widely about the town.

The newspaper called it suicide
Her twin was certain it was not.
Some locals blamed a hobo in town
Traveling for jobs he sought.

Her sister knew she had plans to move
When winter loosed its snowy grasp.
Eagerly she awaited spring.
To be free of there at last.

She'd slit her face, but not her throat
She painted same with dye.
Though on both her tongue and lips
The coroner couldn't lie.

No dye was found in her throat nor
In her intestinal tract
What had killed her was overlooked
And diamond dye became the fact.

Tho' the family screamed of foul play
Her deep religion being their why.
Authorities seemed not to sway
But accepted the coroner's lie.

The strychnine was never opened,
The dye sprinkled across the bed.
The straight razor didn't kill her
And yet they found her dead.

One hundred twenty years have gone
And still, we do not know
Exactly what took place that day.
Nor who or what killed Edith Gerow.

Celeste Q.

Party Time

I'm sick of romance, sick of fear,
Bring on some poems with a little cheer.
No more cracked ribs, no broken hearts
Bring on the pizza, bring on the beer.

Dig out the munchies
Where's the stash?
Bring on the party
Ah ah not that, not the ____.

They'll block you faster than you could run
And all we want is a little fun.
So, we won't bring that no siree
Set your wandering mind at ease.

Most poets write what's in their soul,
This one writes with no control.
I did my soul digging in the past
I've earned a bit of merriment at last!

So, bring on the pizza and the beer.
Spread some laughter and lots of cheer.
Time to lay life's woes aside
Join in life's party and enjoy the ride!

Celeste Q.

The Naked Poet

There's nothing as naked as a poet.
They bare their souls to you.
They open up and let you see
The very blood running through their veins.

There's no one more honest than a poet.
For it's with truth their emotions are inked.
They pen reality as they lived each line
And that is what makes them great.

There's no one more sensitive than a poet.
It's their deepest feelings they portray.
They open up and say "this is who I am."
Oblivious to what the critics may think.

There is no one more vulnerable than a poet.
They've bared their souls, opened their veins,
Allowed total strangers to dissect their brains.
And still, they live to write.

There's no one braver than a poet.
Standing naked on the inside before all.
Dissected, studied, critiqued or praised.
Daring to continue to speak their truths.

Celeste Q.

My Back Yard

I have a piece of heaven
Outside my back door.
There's birds and fish and
Butterflies and bugs and bees galore.

The flowers bloom so beautifully,
The leaves on the trees for shade.
I'm grateful for what God has given me
And the tranquility there displayed.

The fish swim around oblivious
To the birds as they take their bath.
The butterflies flit from bloom to bloom.
Safe from the many birds' wrath.

The scent of the roses leaves me heady
The lilies are a treasure to see.
I spend my days basking in the beauty
Of all that nature provides to me.

So, if you come knocking on my door
You'll know where I can be found.
I'll be in my backyard enjoying the view,
You're welcome to always come around.

Celeste Q.

The Hardest Choice

Have I done enough?
Could I've prolonged it anymore?
Did I do all I could for him?
Then God, why the guilt and so much more?

Why the pain and tears?
Why regrets and such remorse?
Why am I feeling empty,
When it was nature who took its course?

Why am I not happy?
A life of freedom have I to live.
Why do I feel the choices
Were mine, yet were never mine to give?

How should I feel
On this first day of my new life?
This can't be right.
This feeling was to be of laughter not one of strife.

Why am I not tough enough
To walk away, just say goodbye?
Why does your wounded look
Break my heart in pieces and make me want to cry?

God bear my pain,
Lift the chains that now weigh me down.
Shoulder this unfounded guilt,
Please lift my spirits, I can't do this on my own.

Celeste Q.

Today Is Fateday

When days were given names, they misnamed one
They should have named it fateday.
The day your fate becomes a reality,
The day you can no longer run....

It's time to pay the piper day.
Time to pull your own weight.
Time to face up to your past mistakes.
Face the consequences, bear the weight.

Time to accept failure or win.
The day your cards will fall.
Time to give the roulette wheel a spin.
The day that just might end it all.

Yes, we all need a fateday
To clear out the past.
To wake us up and show us
Where we stand at last!

Celeste Q.

My Legacy

If I line my grandchildren in a row,
Oldest to youngest as they grow.
I see myself in every one,
Just little things but my line lives on.

The oldest brings laughter to every day,
The next likes to bake that is her way,
Then there's the one that looks and acts like me.
We have a special bond that all can see.

Attitude surrounds her, she's gone from 1st to 3rd.
Her many talents hidden, few know her worth.
Next is the nature lover close to my heart
Shared interests not DNA yet bonds never part.

Then there's the cool kid that I used to be.
He's followed by the "Rock" the least one like me.
A future football player, from his mother's stock.
He too loves to 4 wheel but he'll likely be a jock.

Now we have the reader, with the sarcastic tongue.
Sharp as a tack with her double-jointed thumbs.
Mr. Encyclopedia reminds me of someone I know
Tidbits of knowledge from his mouth do flow.

The cook and the baker follows close behind.
Short and sweet she is, but with a huge heart so kind.
Her younger cousin follows, his long hair is so fine
He loves to hug tightly so I know he's one of mine.

Then comes his younger brother who races far ahead.
He's never slowed down long enough to see inside his head.
And last there is the toddler with her inquisitive mind.
She is the old soul of the family carrying on the line.

Yes, every one of the dozen, has a part of me
Some things very obvious but some things one can't see.
Each one so precious, makes my heart take flight
I truly am blessed knowing that I did something right.

Celeste Q.

One True Friend

I ran into an acquaintance today
While walking down the street.
She said "Hello, how are you?"
I answered, "Fine thanks."
She said, "That's sweet."

I walked a little further
And a dear friend caught my eye.
She asked, "Cee, how are you?"
I told her I was, "Fine."
She asked, "Then, what is it makes you cry?"

"I'm not crying, I am laughing,
This is me grinning can't you see?"
"Yes" she said, "I see that."
"But I'm not another stranger
Remember? This is me"

She opened up her arms to me
And I pulled her in quite close.
My tears splashed on her cheeks,
Some landing on her nose.

"I guess I just feel lonely. No one
Understands my plight."
But suddenly out of nowhere,
Everything became alright.

Celeste Q.

I Try

My lines aren't straight,
The paint won't flow,
I need new brushes,
But I try.

I can't see straight,
The lights not bright,
My shoulder is stiff,
But I try.

My hands are cramped
I'm getting too old
I can't paint a straight line,
But I try.

My lines are too bold now
It takes twice as long.
To create my fine art.
But I try.

Celeste Q.

Strings

I am not the master,
I do not pull the strings.
I merely write what's in my heart
And see what my words bring.

I do the dance that's played for me,
No choice in the notes I hear.
I write the song, and do the dance
Until the message rings clear.

The words spill out line after line,
I write in desperate measure.
The emotions I release inside your soul,
Are meant to bring you pleasure.

I add some sunlight to a rainy day.
I always bring you laughter.
I try to write your fears away.
Help you find what you are after.

Celeste Q.

Someone Special

Today I met a friend,
Someone that saw through my veneer.
On passed the jokes and laughter
And still he found me dear.

He felt the hurts and sorrows
I've hidden all these years.
He overlooked the bitterness
And brushed away my fears.

I opened up my heart to him,
All the secrets I'd kept here.
He knows me like no other.
He's tasted all my tears.

It is a peaceful feeling
Whenever I find him near.
I pray we'll always be close friends.
He knows I'll always hold him dear.

Celeste Q.

Our Son

In the midst of the night when all was so black,
Something beckoned me outside to my deck.
Up in the east and off to the right
Shone one lonely star with the brightest of lights.

Its twinkle drew my eyes up to the sky.
I thought of you son, knew your spirit was nigh.
It brought a small smile to my tear-stained face.
I returned back inside with a deep inner peace.

Shortly thereafter other people appeared,
All claiming that they'd seen something weird.
Only one star lit the whole sky,
Off to the east and not up very high.

They all thought of you son, on your heavenly flight.
It brought peace to them knowing that you'd be alright.
From both ends of the city we were drawn to this thing
And we knew your spirit was soaring up to your king.

I'm sure you are helping God build a brand-new add-on,
Making sure it's done right with nothing left undone.
You're eating lasagna the angels prepared for your flight,
And you're ordering meatballs from the menu for Saturday night.

(Missing you always)

Celeste Q.

Bye Bye My Canadian Guy

Bye bye my Canadian guy.
Drove his rig to the hill but the funding went dry.
The good ol' boys sat up there on high
Singing this will be the day
Freedoms die.

While JT hides and the puppet's strings get tight,
The green and bloc are in a fright,
And the rest are left to cry out about the site.
And whole wide world stops, holding their breath
But all the liberal's ears are deaf.
The day the freedoms die

Bye bye my Canadian guys.
Held their lines real tight
'Til their options went dry.
The good ol' boys were all
Singing will this be the day freedom dies?

Bye bye my trucking guy.
Drove his big rig to the hill but their voice was denied.
The good old club was screaming the economy's fried.
Yelling this will be the day freedoms die!

The big axe falls as the cops fly in
And the mini pm says with a grin,
"We've got their wallets and assets"
As she holds them high.

The citizens run as they're pushed around.
The vets are shoved down to the ground.
As they all hold their dignity up high.
Weeping "This will be the day freedom dies."

Bye bye my fellow guys,
At least let it be known
That we gave it a try.
So sorry for Canada for exposing the lies
But this will be the day freedoms die

Then out to the east what did they hear?
Suddenly a massive cheer,
As the Quebec truckers are taking up the line.
The trucks rolled in with the light
And horns a blaring to take up their fight.
And all that watched were in delight.
Singing "I don't think this is
the day Freedom dies!
"

Celeste Q.

Helpless

I bleed for you not just tears, but blood tears.
Soul wrenching anguish.
You're here, but now you're gone.
Your future, nothing but a wish.

Your reality of twenty years,
Still fresh in your mind.
But where you sleep and what you just ate
Are ghosts of another time.

Those eyes no longer sparkle just a haze
Where once you lived.
The future you once dreamed of
Now only the past your memories give.

That childlike need you've developed
So out of character for you.
I look at you and I bleed new tears
There is nothing I can do.

I can't repair the damage
That has happened to your mind.
I can't give you back your strength
From another time.

I can't settle all your differences
Nor put those hurts to rest.
They're gone now, forever left undone
In your dark abyss.

I can only help you through this journey,
And try my very best.
To comfort you and support you
While you struggle with the rest.

I can be there for you to lean on
When you're sad, and all alone.
I'll be there by your side to help you
'Til your mind has totally gone.

Celeste Q.

The Game Of Control

I bore this pain for years and yet,
Determined I was not to let
It destroy my goals or my daily life.
Onward I pushed myself through the strife.

Behind closed doors I shed my tears
I blanked my mind to all my fears.
Convinced myself it would pass like a season.
Terrified to know what was the reason.

I worked and partied my way through the pain.
Raised a family - kept active but all was in vain.
Lived life to its fullest and paid the cost.
But in the end, the winner was pain all along and

I accept that I lost.

Celeste Q.

If Tomorrow Starts Without Me

If tomorrow starts without me, smile, it means I'm free.
Don't shed a tear there's no despair.
I'm where I'm meant to be.

If tomorrow starts without me, just know that you were loved.
I gave my heart so freely
And guard yours from up above.

If tomorrow starts without me, then my job is finished here.
I've been rewarded for my work
And God has called me near.

If tomorrow starts without me, never be upset.
I've bore my pain and paid my dues,
And left with no regret.

Celeste Q.

Christmas

There is no time like Christmas,
For laughter, warmth and love.
The good lord smiles down on us
With gentleness from above.

He hears our hopes and answers
All that he possibly can.
His love and understanding
Brings a calmness to the land.

Thank you Lord for Christmas
A day to cherish so.
I'm grateful for this single day,
To spend with ones that I love so.

Celeste Q.

The Artist

Last night in peaceful sleep I thought,
What kind of life it would be
To live with an artist who cared and sought,
True loving sanctimonious harmony.

The hand of time cannot restrain
Those talents born within.
The gifts of God must sustain
And be passed on to all akin.

A mind that is but a seeding bed
Nurtured, watered, and constantly fed.
Yet to reap the fruits that have been sown
The artists truths must be shown.

A freeing of such talents you see
Can turn the seed into a tree.
The tree will blossom and then some day
To the strongest winds it will not sway.

An artist's talents remain untold
Until on paper, their soul unfolds
To stifle such talent is truly unfair
The world must witness such gifted flair.

Go forth and grow and own your gift,
These talents are granted to few.
Let them heal all and repair life's rifts.
Bring forth beauty from all that you do.

Anonymous
(Written with respect for)
Celeste Q.

My Son

The mother of boys has its joys,
Snakes and frogs and tools and toys.
Frogs in jars, but here's the rub,
Watch for snakes slithering in the tub!

Oh well, at least it's not a girl
Or another mean, nasty squirrel.
Hours upon hours of picking up tools,
Cars under feet, stepping on wire spools.

And just when you really lose your cool,
He says "I love you mommy," and oh what a fool.
You feel so ungrounded and soon
You're surrounded In Walmart's tool isle
Just to see his sweet smile.

Celeste Q.

My Friend The Almost Robber

She opened the door to darkness
And little did she know,
That it could well become the day
Her world changed and she didn't know.

She called out first timidly
And then a little louder.
As she stepped into the gloomy room
Things got a little cloudier?

Her instincts yelled, her hair rose up,
Things just weren't seeming right.
She backed outside so quickly.
But couldn't shake the fright.

Across the street she hurried
The bank would know what to do,
But the tellers were too busy,
For they only employed a few.

She saw the cops arriving and
She wanted to explain,
But by the time she got there
None of them remained.

Knowing that her fingerprints
were the latest on the scene,
She pondered what she should do
Without her being seen.

At last, she went to the cops
Turning herself in.
They questioned her gently
Then met her with a grin.

The place was not robbed that day.
It seems no one wanted furs.
The owner had walked away
Forgetting to lock his doors!

Celeste Q.

Custody

"I love you Daddy," the little boy said.
And Daddy grinned and patted his head.
"I love you too son," he said with a smile.
Then he turned his face away for a while.

"The very best present I could get when I'm eight
Is to live with you Dad. I really can't wait.
I pray to God but he can't hear me,
And my brother does too, but he's only three"

But Daddy is stuck in a living hell,
He's sworn as a parent some truths to not tell.
To encourage this desire would instill false hope.
So as his tears slide, he wonders how he will cope.

Then the house looms before them and he wipes off their tears.
As he loosens their grasping arms, he questions their fears.
He wonders if it's normal not to want to see Mom.
But he's not able to ask him, his son still sucks his thumb.

So, he tries to calm them and banish their worry.
And he promises this week will go by in a hurry.
"Before you know it, you'll be seeing me again."
But inside he's crying, he can feel their pain.

As he drives out of sight his heart fills with despair.
So, he too prays to God if there is one somewhere.
He prays that the pain his sons feel will ease.
And he prays his dream will be answered as God should please.

And he wonders if this is really in the best interest of the child,
Or some powerful system that is just running wild.
If this is so right, why are they all living such hell?
And he knows there's no answer
Only time will tell.

Celeste Q.

Freedom

Very few people have glimpsed into my soul.
By isolating others, I've put myself in control.
I've molded me and shaped me
To be as I am today.
There's been very little outside help
For which I must repay.

No, I have no obligations to my friends, no debts to be repaid.
I did all of this on my own, for this freedom I have slaved.
Free to be whom and what I want,
A lucky person I am now.
Independence I have gained
And it's just myself, I owe.

Free of gifts at Christmas- no hustle and bustle for me.
While you're out shopping frantically, I'm watching my T.V.
Free of birthdays that I must remember
No showers to be attended.
While weaker hearts may be shattered,
Mine will never need to be mended.

Free to come home to my place and toss things where I may
No justification necessary, for the right I need not pay.
Free to choose whatever I wish to do,
To come home whenever I might.
To stay in and accomplish things
Or party out all night!

Free to drive my car with fury or treat it with kidskin gloves.
To pick and choose what I wish to do. No compromise for love.
Free to procrastinate when I feel like,
To overlook unpleasant chores.
There's but one single freedom eluding me,
To trade this lonely life for yours!

Celeste Q.

Christmas Ghost

I hang the ghosts of Christmas past upon my unclothed tree.
With everyone I hang so gently, they smile back at me.
Their dreams and hopes and wishes all encased in the glass.
I'm hanging all their futures that will never come to pass.

The ones that went before me but left a trinket rare.
I hang each memory one at a time and with the utmost care.
I see all their faces clearly in the recess of my mind.
And I smile at the memories they left here for me to find.

The flood of warmth I feel as I gaze upon my tree,
Never fails to amaze me. Friends and family do I see.
The times we enjoyed are oft forgotten throughout the year
But suddenly rejuvenate and again are crystal clear.

I cry when one gets broken, it's a life forever gone.
But I tidy up the pieces knowing their spirit still lives on.
And I wonder just how many more Christmases will be
Before my memory will be all that's left, hanging on this tree.

Celeste Q.

Mom (Post Trauma)

MOM (post trauma)

As a toddler, I needed you

As a child, I played with you

As a teenager, I abhorred you

As an adolescent, I tolerated you

As an adult, I respected you

As a mature woman, I wished that I was like you

As a senior, I realize I have become the new you.

Celeste Q.

Bubbling Brook

My mind is a bubbling brook of poems
Flowing endlessly.
For every one I manage to pen,
I've forgotten at least three.

The words come in and form a line
And everything sounds so very fine.
And then they're gone into the blue,
The ones retained are but a few.

I need a recorder in my mind
To preserve the poems that I can't find.
They've left me in a hurried flash
Before my pen could do its task.

Gone once more from whence they came.
And I have only myself to blame.
I did not keep my pen on hand
Nor paper to catch words as they land.

My recorder is broken, not replaced
My gigabytes are used, there is no space.
So, the bubbling brook of poems flows endlessly
And one day, may well become a sea.

Celeste Q.

Shoveling Snow's Musing

It all started with my back
"This shoveling is killing me" it screamed.
Of course, my heart pipes up with "but I don't want to die
Until I've known true love."
This opened the door for my soul to step in. "But you have known true
love.
I've loved you since before time"
"I know that", said my heart, "but I mean the passion and caring of
human love."
Of course, then my spirit had to get into the act. Of course.
Spunky as always. "Well, I don't know what the problem is.
You're all gloom and doom. There's work to be done."
Worry about your passions and inside parts later,
For now, just shovel snow!"

Celeste Q.

Category 2

Spiritual/Soul growth

Oh Lord I Pray

God take away this loneliness,
Guide me through my time of stress.
Bring true love home to me
Sheltered and guided through eternity.

Make my soul be a part of them.
Carry us in your hands unto the end.
Help us as we tarry along life's road.
Please carry this heavy burdened load.

Please somewhere in this stress and gloom
Give me strength to lighten a darkened room.
Mark these words down as my spiritual prayer.
Unto you my Lord I have placed my care.

Celeste Q.

The Price

Sometimes late at night, I ponder life
In the still dark hours alone.
I realize the consequences of living
Are mine to pay on my own.

There really isn't anything or one
That can make my decisions for me.
At night it hits home, when I'm
totally alone
That 'tis I must pay my fees.

No Friends, nor money, nor
activities
Allow me to procrastinate forever.
Eventually I must face my life
It's costs to pay, I must endeavor.

In tears and pain, oh yes, we learn
That we alone must pay the price.
The cost of this thing we cherish,
This frivolous thing we call life.

So, tread gently and treat it not
lightly.
Absolution is not easily earned.
And the haunting returns to you
nightly.
'Tis a lesson better avoided than
learned.

Celeste Q.

Just The Puppet

I am not the creator.
I do not pull the strings.
I merely do the puppet's
Dance, and endure
Whatever life brings.

I say and write what he
Tells me
I do just as I'm told.
I often question "why me?"
So far, I've not been told.

I can't foresee the future,
I cannot erase the past.
I only dance in the present
And trust the strings hold fast.

Celeste Q.

Dreams And Wishes

I've wanted for many years now,
But never got too far.
I would have got much farther had
I wished upon a star.

Maybe if I had a rabbit's foot
Or a lucky coin or two,
A four-leaf clover or shamrock,
An old horseshoe might do.

I'm not too sure what it would take
To make my dreams come true.
I've been told that lots of elbow grease
And much hard work will do.

I've stocked as much elbow grease
As my poor cupboards will hold.
But now I hear 'tis timing does the trick
At least that's what I'm told.

Proof of my years of hard work
Is here waiting to be told.
But now I've heard that all it takes
Is a pencil lined with gold.

You see what I've always wished for,
And just cannot seem to do,
Is write a book about my life
And show my real self to you.

Celeste Q.

Your Ghost

Did you see me today?
When you looked into your mirror?
Did you gaze into my eyes
And see the other side of you?

Did you not realize why I'm here?
The reflection of all you're missing?
I'm not here to look good and feed your pride,
I'm here to point out your flaws.

I have no ego as you've claimed it all.
No heart, as you've locked it behind your wall.
I've no money, you have enough of that.
No time as you've channeled every second.

No pride will you see here. You're the lion,
I'm but the reflection in your mirror.
I've no conditions, you took those away.
No future, those contracts never go away.

Are you proud of what you see there?
Do you feel the balance and love?
Do you languish in your reflection?
Does admiration swell your chest?

Do you dare look closer, to your soul?
To the depths from which you run?
Do you languish in the beauty of me
Or does your guilt repel you back?

Slow down take a closer look.
I have qualities, all your lost ones.
The ones you've tried to push from your mind.
The ones you now can't seem to find.

I have imagination and creativity.
I can draw a whole future of love and home
With just one minute of time and affection.
I can mold a heart with just one tear.

I can construct, I can build a whole life
With just one second of your time.
And time - that, I have lots to share
As I wait in this mirror world alone.

I can give unconditional love.
You left me none when you set yours in stone.
I can give all the free things in life.
Those unimportant things like love.

The smiles of happiness, walks in nature,
Laughter, cuddling, sharing, true caring.
I have an abundance of these free things.
I've been storing them here in your mirror.

I can give you patience and understanding
My mirror is overflowing with those,
While I'm trapped here waiting for you
To have the courage to look closer.

Celeste Q.

Through the Lens Backwards

Today I looked backward through a
telescope.
With much bewilderment did I see.
Tiny dots running back and forth
through time,
Mere specks in infinity.

Mere particles of dust rushing
endlessly
Toward some invisible goal.
The fruits of their labor too miniscule
to see,
Too busy to pay heed to their souls.

Then I glanced up to the gates of
heaven .
There stood a man who'd toiled and
slaved.
And yet he had nothing to show for
his life
His possessions, millions of light
years away.

His house and his car far too tiny to
see
By the strongest telescopic eye.
The cottage he'd toiled for all of his life
Went unseen as the telescope passed by.

I watched as he waited in line for admission.
And I felt the futility of his life.
As he glanced over his shoulder toward his home
I saw a face that reflected much inner strife.

He crumpled as he realized what he'd worked for,
Was too far to purchase his entry there.
The one possession he was allowed to bring with him
Was his soul, but alas it was empty and bare.

When I realized he'd toiled for eighty odd years,
With compassion I tried to help him all I could.
But the gap between us was far too wide to bridge
And my efforts, though well intended, did no good.

As he turned from the gates so rejected
My heart filled with such hopeless despair.
Though too late for him, the lesson I'd learned
With others I knew I must share.

My telescope is here free to borrow.
To remind you of what makes you whole.
So, when you get to the gates of heaven,
You'll be proud of what's in your soul.

Celeste Q.

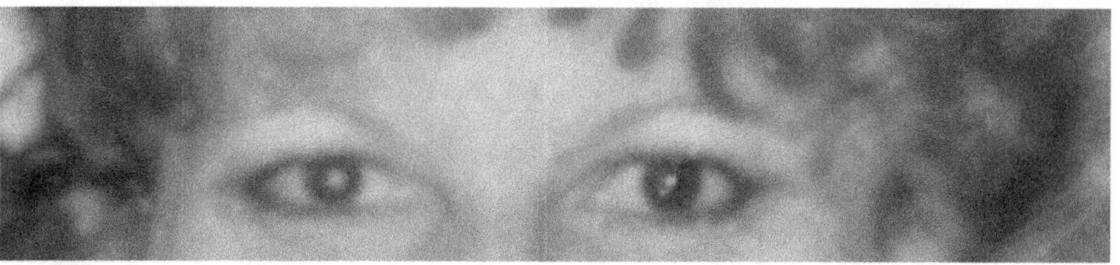

Tired Eyes

Too much life has passed by these eyes.
Too much pain and too many lies.
Too many times they've begged for naught.
Too tired from looking for the path they sought.

Too swollen from crying for other's pains.
Too weary to search for my own self gains.
Too scared from all the things they see.
Too shy to show the real me.

Too blurry from the lack of sleep.
Too bloodshot from the tears I weep.
Too caring for the needs of others.
Too guilty when I can't be bothered.

Too dreary from burning the candle both ends.
Too timid from trying to make amends.
Too blinded from the screens I see.
Too angry because of life's deceits.

Too green from envy-your time I share.
Too frigid to pretend I even care.
Too innocent like a child at play.
Too cloudy like the clouds today.

Too droopy from the books I read.
Too hungry for the love I need.
Too dressed up trying to impress.
Too, too, too, I just need rest.

Celeste Q.

Mother

I know well that I owe you for
The first eighteen years of my life.
But did you not once stop to think
We could have lived with a lot less strife?

Fewer insults - no jibes would have been nice
A lot less criticism and ridicule.
I've far excelled the normal standards
But I still feel like such a fool.

I was not allowed to grow in peace,
My own worst critic so they say.
Always striving for perfection
And falling short along the way.

I've accomplished much in this lifetime
With my unending passion to succeed.
My compulsion to improve myself
Not a hunger, but a need.

There's no pat upon my shoulders,
No proud strut nor braggart's sway.
I'll never reach perfection
Try as I might each day.

You've set my standards too high.
A goal, I'll never quite reach.
You've left me always striving,
A student, never good enough to teach.

Forever an underachiever
Never worthy of anyone's love.
Always anticipating condemnation
To be passed down from above.

Now don't take this wrong - I'm thankful
For all you've done for me.
But could I ask for one more favor?
The compliment that will set me free!

Celeste Q.

Then I Found The Box

I've written my poems since early days
And stored them out of sight.
I penned my life as I went on my way
Never running out of things to write.

I wrote of love, motherhood and tears
I journaled all my childhood fears.
Whenever life got in my way
I put it to paper where it would stay.

Years passed by; poems went untouched.
The box grew dusty, not opened much.
It fell out of sight, out of thought and mind.
All of my poems were left far behind.

Until today - I found the box.

I opened it and out poured the hurt.
My childhood pains I tried to skirt.
The adolescent fantasies,
Dreams of youth and what could be.
They all laid bare their painful truth,
Gone are the days of my youth.

Then came the change I'd travelled through
The painful days of me and you.
The tears fell down like acid rain
But I could not close the box again.

I gave it voice - it gave me strength.
I read each poem at some length.
Feeling the torments that caused my write,
Turning my daylight back into night.

I felt each poem, I relived my life
And every cut from each sharp knife.
I placed them back. Picked up the locks
One last time I closed the box.

Celeste Q.

Earning Eternity

So many times, I've offered my soul
To replace someone's unknown.
God wouldn't take me and spare their life
He said I had work left undone.

I've searched for my purpose both inside and out,
Examined both emotions and thoughts.
I asked for guidance on this work left undone.
Drew a blank from the things I've been taught.

I questioned the sorrow I felt for other's strife,
I dreaded my tomorrows - would gladly give my life.
I toiled through each day, living in pain.
The answers eluded me; my search was in vain.

What is my purpose that I haven't quite learned
What torture must I live before eternity is earned
Death doesn't scare me as I know it should
But living my life without love and hope, surely would.

Could that be my purpose? Why God's left me here?
Is this the message of his that I see crystal clear?
Am I to write of his love, his kindness and grace?
And pray those who read will wish to change their ways?

Can I show them that love is the glue that binds?
That saves our future, the fate of mankind?
How do I compare it to that devastating state,
That follows on the heels of unadulterated hate?

Celeste Q.

I've Lost My Smile

I see the pictures of yesteryear.
And suddenly it's crystal clear.
I've dallied here for too long awhile,
Sheltered my heart, but lost my smile.

Protected myself from all life's pain,
But in the end what did I gain?
Shielded myself from the hurt and tears.
But now I'm left with far greater fears.

So many years I let pass me on by,
Not wanting to love or give life a try.
Old age is approaching all too fast
And I'm but a memory in someone's past.

Celeste Q.

This Poet's Job

I am but a basic poet,
No fancy words from me.
I Merely write of how I feel
And what I truly see.

I did not come as Joan of Arc
To save the world from loss.
I was not born in Salem
Or to burn upon a cross.

I wasn't meant to hang alone
For all the world to see.
I was put here on this earth
To help you set your spirit free.

I laugh, I sing, I paint, I dance
Not much to me at a glance,
But look a little deeper
Past the laughter and the mirth.
You'll see a lot of wisdom
I've gathered from this earth.

I've packed a lot of living
In the years that I've been here.
I've had a lot of good times
And shed my share of tears.

I've dreamed a million lifetimes
To do mankind some good.
To pen my truths and spread the light
Bringing hope as healers should.

Celeste Q.

The Perfect Child

When someone's angry with me it's like I was a child.
They speak cruel words to me and suddenly
I'm getting my fingers slapped by my mother
In front of her friends, who are chiding me,
And scolding me and embarrassing me into being
The perfect child.

The tears well up inside me. The lump in my throat
And the ache in my chest threatens to explode.
But the determination in my soul guides me.
And I refuse to show the hurt. After all, I am
The perfect child.

I've grown in both size and years it's true, but still
I'm lost somewhere inside. Forever trapped with
My hand, still in the cookie jar. Always afraid
Of onlookers scolding me, embarrassing me into being
The perfect child.

And Though I've tried like never before in my life,
To be everything anyone could wish to be and more,
The times I fall short as I often do, and I know I have
Let someone down. I forget that to err is human. I should be
The perfect child.

I chide myself and try to correct the wrongs,
To figure out what I did to upset and what I could do
To repair the damage and never repeat my mistake.
This tortured mind is the product of what should have been
The perfect child.

Celeste Q.

When I Was The Victim

You may say it's good to be out of there
Away from him and free.
If so, then why don't I feel that way?
It's never ending can't you see?
I used to have a sense of humor
I was happy and carefree.
I'd laugh and talk and carry on,
An out- going personality.

But now I'm trapped inside myself
My life is a joke no more.
The controlling hand, though invisible
Is there just like before.
The bruises faded and now are gone,
The tears at last have dried.
Yet the pain inside grows worse now
Because a part of me has died.

Am I all alone? Does no one feel
The abuse that I've lived through?
Does no one see or understand
That in its wake lies a residue?
How quick they have forgotten
The woman I used to be.
They think this bitter cutting tongue
Is really truly me?

What has become of all my past
When life was a merry -go-round?
Where laughter, music and singing
Were such familiar sounds?
I truly thought that I'd escaped
And could turn my life around,
But the extent of damage that was done
Has left me totally bound.

I'm forever a prisoner to that hell
Never to forget or pretend.
While outwardly I appear quite well
Inside I question if I'll ever mend.
When will I react to things normally?
With a shrug instead of tears?
Will I ever be strong emotionally?
And not haunted by the fears?

Will I be free to live my life
The way I did before?
Or will I always be condemned
To be his victim forever more?
Oh yes, I'm free of his abuse,
I've left, divorced and more.
But no one seems to realize
It doesn't stop when one shuts the door.

Now fear is my steady companion
And nightmares sleep with me.
The icicles squeeze around my heart
When his face I think I see.
The phone that dies when I say "Hello"
The police car down the street.
The bigger kids on Halloween
Just waiting to trick or treat.

The little things that you pass by
And you never seem to see,
Are major threats that control my life.
Catastrophes to me.
Oh yes, I'm still his victim
I'm reminded every day.
I wait in anticipation
Wondering when he'll make me pay.

I dry my tears, I smile and laugh
And pretend that I'm truly free.
Yet inside I'm praying for someone
To restore my faith in humanity.

Celeste Q.

Know Me By Name.

I am always deeply offended by the term "victim."
A word that implies that someone at some time had control of me.
To correct by following up with the term "survivor" adds to the affront.
That means from the victim point forward my whole being is
But a label of their control, still active, still controlling.

So, what should you refer to me as, you may ask?
I am me. Despite the pain, despite the terrors, despite the
Loneliness, the struggles, the feelings of unworthiness,
I am me. Call me by name. Know me by my name.
Know me by my heart, by my life's lessons. See me as I have become.

See that I have grown and outgrown that person of yesteryear.
Know that the pain of the past was merely a learning curve.
That I have learned the necessary lessons and have moved on.
That I've released the negativity and embraced the future.
And still, I can open my heart, wide open, trusting and lovingly.

No, never again think of me as a victim nor a survivor.
Think of me as a Healer, for I have healed and I love.
I love my past lessons, I love my person, I love life.
Unafraid, unabashed, unlimited and unconditionally.
I am whole, my heart is pure. It is open. Unafraid to beat again.

Celeste Q.

Remorse

I stand alone in the darkness
Watching as life passes me by.
I've given up on understanding
The reasons why I cry.

I cry for all the undreamed dreams
That were never meant to be.
Ambitions and glorious future,
The past that will never be.

I cry for the things lost before
That didn't belong to me.
Success, fame and laughter,
Of belonging somewhere - you see.

I cry for the innocent childhood
That was destroyed so easily.
I cry for this pain that traps me so,
And will never set me free.

As I stand here alone in the darkness
Watching life pass me by
'Tis because I'm too scared to take a chance
That really makes me cry.

Celeste Q.

The Rabbit Holes

I don't play games with people's minds.
There's too many rabbit holes to find.
I go down one and then another
Until I get lost or too tired to bother.

If I can't find the way back- should I go on?
I'm so alone and afraid, still I try to be strong.
Overthinking this and overthinking that,
It blinds me and the paths have all gone black.

I navigate slowly picking my path,
Wondering with each turn will this be my last?
Will the glow of my home light finally show?
Or will I trap myself down here and never know?

So do unto others as you'd have them do.
An over thinker's rabbit holes are more than a few.
They leave me thinking that I'm all alone
And I wonder will I ever find the way home?

Celeste Q.

Mellowing

My lines aren't straight as they used to be.
My eyes don't see like they used to see
My brushes are old and the bristles not long
My paint won't flow, the glide is gone.

Where once my lines were black and white
Clean as day and dark as night
They've learned to curve and bend a little
To meet diversity in the middle.

My eyes don't look like they used to look
I see the lines of life aren't in a book.
Symmetry has flown out the door
The balance of life is no more.

Celeste Q.

Storms Of Life

Many days I drifted back through the infinity of time.
To a life once lived in endless greed and a love that wasn't mine.
The rivers roared, the earth shook, the tremors deep in my soul.
The senseless time that was wasted by the clamoring of a fool.

To span the endless time and space with a bridge of solid gold
Took the power of a volcanic eruption to free me from its hold.
Traditions tossed and values altered with the speed of a hurricane's wind.
He who weathered the storms to the end, was he who would ultimately
win.

When the storm subsides, in the aftermath there's a certain calm within.
I've finally crossed over that bridge of gold, now a new life can begin.
The signs of pain and lines of strife have diminished from my face.
Replaced by a smile of love and peace, self-worth stands now in its
place.

Never to return to the life I lived, the storms were far too violent then.
This inner peace and calm I've found, is far better than hate within.
Yet still I calm the last of the storm, though the hurricane has gone,
I fill my days with pleasant thoughts, and pray for strength to carry on.

Celeste Q.

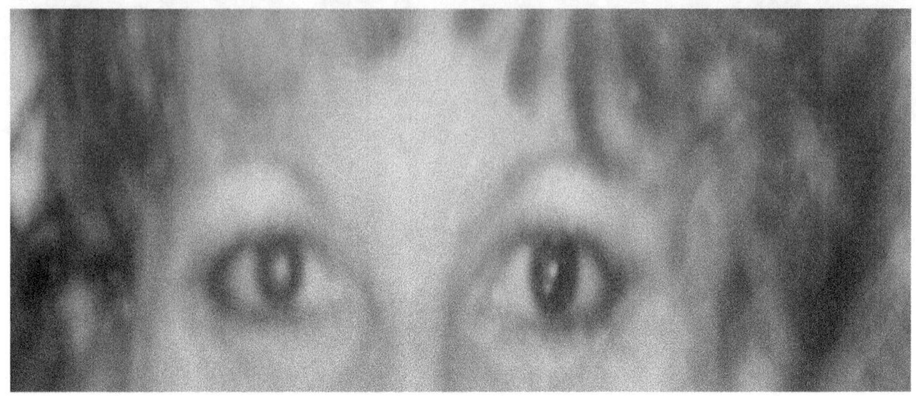

A Stranger's Eyes

Will I still see the same
When you take out my eyes?
Will I still see the truths in life
And discern them from the lies?

Will there still be rainbows
On dreary rainy days?
Will my sun shine bright
Or will you take that away?

Will I still look the same
When you replace them with new
Will they still be green
Or will they be brown?
Please, not blue.

Will I see my true love
While I still have my own?
In case I can't recognize him
Through one's that are unknown.

Will you still be able to see
Clearly into my soul or
Will the new eyes leave it
Trapped in total turmoil?

Will I still see life
As I always did before?
Or will I see it as a stranger
And hate what is in store?

Tell me Will I still see the same
When you take out my eyes?

Celeste Q.

My Other Side

Rescue me from this Hell.
Don't force me to go on.
The pain in which I'm forced to dwell
To another's soul belongs.

This isn't my life, not my strife,
Though at times I cannot tell.
Do I bring these feelings on my own
Or is my life, but a wishing well?

I pray for guidance, pray for peace,
Pray for another's plight.
My worries rob me of gentle sleep.
The horrors haunt my nights.

When at my worst I laugh and joke
No one sees my pain.
I pack my sorrows deep inside
And give back love in vain.

Celeste Q.

Paper Doll World

I'm not just a pretty girl
Dressed up in this plastic world,
Draping on your arm
Like some kind of lucky charm.

I'm a person with a soul
With a huge heart and a mind.
Not a wind-up you control
Or some toy that you just find.

You can't wind me up and flaunt me.
Build your ego at my cost.
You can't strut me like a token
Then leave me to get lost.

Love me for the real me,
Take time to look inside.
Have the courage to get to know me
A privilege most are denied.

Treat me as a real human
That cries and bleeds and sweats.
I'm not plastic, I'm not a barbie,
I'm a person with regrets.

Understand that in my real world
There's no room for plastic folk.
I left all that behind me when
The phoniness became a joke.

Celeste Q.

Lifelines

These are not wrinkles you see on my face,
They're lifelines direct to my soul.
Each one bares a story in a day of my life
Combined they're what makes me whole.

There's those that are laughter and those that are tears.
Days of excitement and others of fear.
Nights filled with romance days marked by strife
But each is a special part of my life.

So, touch if you wish but please put them back
These creases are pieces of me.
I can't bear to lose one, they can't be replaced
For each is a cherished memory.

They're what makes me whole, the roadmap to my soul
These wrinkles are priceless-not free.
I wear them with pride, there's no need to hide,
They're all part of what makes me- me.

Ty Blink
Celeste Q.

My Past Life

Do you ever dream of Scotland? The castle by the sea?
Do you ever dream of Scotland? Then perhaps you dream of me.
The grounds where we once laughed and played
When there was you and me.

The basalt columns rising up along the castle's side?
The basalt columns baubling up and down gently with the tide.
Where we would hop from one to one
Racing with the tide.

The castle turret rising almost to the sky?
The castle turret's staircase of stone climbing up so high.
Where we would sit for hours watching seabirds soar.
When there was you and I.

Do you ever dream of Scotland? Is this picture in your eye?
In a different world, an early time that scholars will deny.
Do you remember a young lass falling?
Then perhaps you saw me die.

Celeste Q.

Your Wakeup Call

In deep despair these eyes look out
On a world wrapped up in vanity.
Racing, chasing dreams of wealth,
No compassion for humanity.

The days go on like in a song,
'Til finally the last notes played.
Then is the time to tally the cost
And see that the piper's been paid.

Were the nights of pleasure you enjoyed
Truly what made you feel whole?
Are the days of laughter that you ran after
There now to help fill your soul?

Will you treasure all your material things?
When you're taking your very last breath?
Do you welcome what the next life brings
As you look into the eyes of death?

Celeste Q.

Chaos Conspiracies And Quests

Out of the labyrinth of conspiracies
Sprung Chaos fearless and bold.
A mighty disruption in the perfect world
With a past best left untold.

It spewed forth conflicting stories.
Twisting minds and hearts alike.
It basked in all its glories
And relished the chaotic site.

For years it reigned unchallenged,
There was no worthy foe.
It trampled all the beauty in this world
Wherever it chose to go.

Then one day from the labyrinth
A tiny spark appeared.
Unnoticed by those around it
It remained unchallenged and unfeared.

It grew in strength and magnitude
Till it outshone the very sun.
Not a person even realized
Its Quest had just begun.

It came to conquer chaos,
Put conspiracies to bed.
To clear the hearts of turmoil,
The pain in every head.

It brought such a warming comfort
Wherever it chose to flow.
Conspiracies soon disappeared
Where, no one seemed to know.

The Quest was so successful
It was blessed from up above.
Chaos and Conspiracies were defeated.
By one tiny spark called Love.

Celeste Q.

Life in Retrospect

Sometimes in the wee still hours of the night
One ponders life, not knowing wrong from right.
What is the purpose of this life we've been given?
What else is it good for, if not just for living?

Often we fail to look at it in retrospect.
Making wrong choices, justifying-what the heck?
Perhaps if we looked with a different point of view,
The mistakes that we made would be but a few.

As a child we grow wondering what will or won't be.
We hope and we pray, but we really cannot see.
Where our future is taking us we truly don't know,
But we hold onto what feels good and thus do we grow.

As an adult we find that our choices have been made.
Our futures lie before us, the path's been pre-paved.
Now we question how that youth from so many years ago
Could decide for us our future and the road that we must hoe.

Was it him or guilt that wrapped our future up so beautifully?
Am I locked in with my hands tied or free to live my life for me?
That adolescent can't live my life now for he's no longer who I am.
I've changed along the way some grown up, become a man.

And so it is with retrospect that I must live today,
For when my future is my past, it's that for which I'll pay.
Material things won't matter, nor how others would live my life.
Those judges won't be there, only regrets will cause me strife

No, I must live my future as the past it'll be one day
So when it's all that's left, I'll be happy with the price I had to pay.
I'll look back on this one chance I had to live this life for me
And let it go with no regrets, but many beautiful memories.

Celeste Q.

Nature's Co-dependency

How beautifully the rose does bloom
Next to the Scottish thistle.
Their thorny branches intertwine
Yet neither blows the whistle.
They bask in the sun's warmth
And devour the earth's food,
Intent on their tasks to survive.
Paying no heed to each other's jabs,
Just grateful to be alive.

How happy is the cold bleak moon
To forever chase the sun.
Around the earth in an infinite race,
Still following when the day is done.
Always willing to come in second best,
Never welcomed like the sun's warm rays.
Always showing his best face when chased away
By another of sun's warm sunny days.
Just grateful to revolve.

How constantly the river flows
Never ceasing throughout time.
Gently eroding its luscious banks
But earth doesn't seem to mind.
It plucks the odd tree from earth's cover
And a precious gem here and there at random.
They give and take down through the ages
Yet never each other do they abandon.
Just grateful to survive.

How beautiful it would be
If man could survive like the rose,
Living next door to a prickly thorn.
Never minding being second best like the moon,
Giving and taking like the river and shore.
Never weighing up life's daily costs.
Knowing over time the price was miniscule
And by doing so life's purpose would be lost.
Just grateful to have lived.

Celeste Q.

Category 3

True Love

Every Night

Every night to God I pray
That here inside my arms you'll stay.
The roads been rough
The trip's been long,
When I'm with you I know I'm strong
Enough to face life.

Every night to God I pray
That I will please you in every way.
That though there's tears
And though there's pain
You'll come to me to escape the rain,
And I can comfort you.

Every night to God I pray
That we can share just one more day.
We'll, laugh together
Well cry some too,
But we're still together
When the day is through.
And you will hold me.

Every night to God I pray
For your love, the price I'll gladly pay.
That I'll be all you ever need,
That in your heart I will succeed
To please you darling all through our lives.
And you will always love me.

Celeste Q.

The Pit

The quicksand under my feet lies still,
Calm, barely breathing, disguised as hope.
Waiting for me to take that first step.
To make the mistake of letting go.
Take the first last step.

I gaze down on it and I see it's
Shallow breathing, I feel it's pulse.
Slowly but with certainty slithering
Up my torso, searching for a perfect
Place to attach it's deadly tentacles.

I feel it's warmth disguised as love.
And I let it embrace me, croon to me.
Ooze into my veins filling my body
And my heart. Serenading my soul
As it cools and hardens.

And I see it for what it truly is,
Not hope, not love, but an engulfing
Pit of darkness, smiling sweetly.
Lying patiently awaiting it's pray.
With its false welcoming face.

And I take that first last step.
The anticipated step of finality.
Knowing what lies beneath,
Knowing the depth of the pit that awaits
Yet, accepting its false embrace.

Knowing that without hope and love
All is futile and lost regardless.
There is no meaning in an empty life
I take the step, release the fear and
Pray the pit is bottomless and hungry enough.

Celeste Q.

Love

Love is a passion, a state of the mind.
It comes not from the possessions of time.
It's a heartfelt feeling deep in your soul
That makes one smile and literally glow.

Love is a hug, a glance or a stare.
Love is a kiss, a stroke of the hair.
Love is a touch that tingles the spine.
Love is a warmth that sparkles like wine.

Love is a word in the wee hours of the night.
Love is the calming of another's plight.
Love is two hands that gently caress.
Love is a hope for eternal bliss.

Love is a friend, a passionate mate.
Love is the mender of all we hate.
Love is eternity that two people share.
Love allows no one to infringe on them there.

Love is the voice that is silently ornate.
Love is a feeling not an inherited trait.
Love has more value than silver or gold.
Love can never be bought or sold.

Love will come freely, look no more.
From out of the blue it will knock on your door.
Like trees that blossom before they're ready to bare,
True love will bloom year after year.

Celeste Q.

It Just Is

"Will you be my forever?"
My darling asks of me.
How to answer his question?
In a way that he might see.

Why do the birds fly freely,
Yet animals walk the ground?
Why do the stars flare brightly,
Before they plummet down?

Why do the mountains stand so tall?
Rugged yet majestically.
What is it that puts a sparkle,
On even the smallest sea?

How many sands in the desert?
Why can I not see a sound?
Why is the earth not flat like a map?
But nearly perfectly round.

There are so many unsolved questions
Whose answers remain a mystery.
God made everything for a reason
Just accept - "It was meant to be."

Celeste Q.

My Love's Lullaby

My lover flies by angel's wings
Guarded over raging seas.
Forever cradled in their arms
'Til he's safely home with me.

Tho' miles apart our hearts still sing
That ageless symphony,
That hearts entwined forever beat
With true love's harmony.

"Come home to me my other half,
Come home to find your rest.
Let me hold you in my arms
And sleep upon my breast."

I'll hold you in your troubled times.
A gentle lullaby I will sing.
I'll cherish you and all you are
'Til your last flight on angel's wings.

Celeste Q.

I Love You

Last night you said "I love you
And I need you so."
It was the first time ever
That I'd heard it spoken so.

In the midst of our upheaval,
And the words I said so cruel.
You spoke so openly and honestly
That I felt like such a fool.

I never felt the absolute reality
Of those same words before,
All the unspoken feelings they portray
Your love - but so much more.

The absurdity of our argument
Slapped me in the face.
It's reason and its purpose
Was gone without a trace.

You sat there and your sad brown eyes
Said more than words could say.
The fight was lost - your love had won
The cards weren't mine to play.

There never was a choice,
To continue was a lie.
Forgiving you - the payment
For what I'd been given by your eyes.

The truth and the reality
That I never really knew,
I learned it all last night with just
One softly spoken...
"I love you."

Celeste Q.

Always Knew

I always knew there was something missing,
Something tangible that I couldn't put my finger on
Something just out of reach.
That constant feeling that I just don't belong.

I always knew this life wasn't mine, wasn't meant to be.
I shunned the opportunities, shunned the fame.
Not my desire, not my life.
That lingering knowledge of something missing.

I always knew that I didn't belong in this space
Always aware of the loneliness even in the crowds.
That I could do much better,
When others praised, I saw my imperfections.

I always knew I could strive for perfection but I didn't.
Donating what wealth I could amass, it wasn't needed
This life was temporary- not mine,
Killing time, yearning, aching, waiting, longing for...

I always knew, the endless searching for the puzzle piece
The connection, the completion of my soul, my anchor
Tomorrow's dream just out of sight.
The continuous search, the elusive path...

I always knew that in some lifetime it awaited me.
The one with the fame I'd always shunned, the glory I evaded
The warmth I'd always longed for
The gentle encouragement, the ballast, the balance, my yang
It was you; I always knew.

Celeste Q.

Yesterday I Cried

Yesterday I cried, I drank, I pounded out my tunes.
Not from getting jilted, au contraire,
But my love wanted me to join him.
And I couldn't meet him there.

Yesterday I couldn't meet him in the middle tho' I love him so.
I chose honor, dignity and principles,
And risked having to let him go.
I just couldn't join him there.

Yesterday I grew some, inside where shadows loom
And I realized something new to me.
That principles change and dignity is defined by one's own mind.
But it was too late to meet him there.

Yesterday I learned that honor only comes with honesty.
To deny my love was a dishonor to both he and I.
That love is the catalyst of life - All encompassing.
And today I will be waiting for him there.

Celeste Q.

Why

Why am I not happy? When my heart is pounding so?
Why does life get in the way and never let you go?
Why do we complicate our days like they'll be an endless flo?
Tell me why am I not happy? I really do not know.

Why am I not jumping when you're all I'd ever need?
Why am I worried about your monetary greed?
Why do I need more time to consider your offer? Oh, so rare.
Tell me why? I love you to the core of me and am I being fair?

Why do birds not sing? When you're all that life could bring.
Why am I tied in knots? You've always been my everything.
Why am I now so insecure? I really do not know.
Tell me why? I'm scared to commit yet cannot let you go?

Why did you see past my jokes and deep inside my soul?
Why did you keep returning? Until I lost control?
Why were you so addictive like an illegal hit?
Tell me why? I didn't look for cupid's arrow but I sure felt it hit.

Why did I not run to you as in every other past life?
Why is this dilemma causing me so very much strife?
Why am I suffering so, and wallowing in such pain?
Tell me why I am so terrified to connect with my twin flame.

Celeste Q.

Unconditional Love

Knows no restrictions, no limits, no boundaries.
Unconditional love
Lays their heart in your hand
Then slices it in two and trades half for half of your own.
They know it is safe because you won't harm it
You depend on it now to help your own beat true.

Unconditional love
Knows that you're human and forgives human mistakes.
Unconditional love
Has learned from their own and will never judge yours,
Nor will they question, but rather wait for you to share.
To err is human and one must be human to accept such love.
You can be just that, yourself, in their presence.

Unconditional love
Will never turn elsewhere for attention or love.
Unconditional love
Knows there is no one else, you own their soul.
Their heart is sewn to yours permanently.
It beats only for you, because of you.
When times are the toughest both hearts are safe.

Unconditional love
Is the rarest blessing one can receive on earth.
Unconditional love
Needs no ego, no pride they've outgrown such.
They've survived life's harshest lessons.
When it is given, it is given through knowledge.
They know without doubts, you deserve.

Unconditional love
Comes only to those who are on a higher spiritual level.
Unconditional love
Is eternal, a reward, a pillar of strength, a guide,
Given only to those that would never abuse it.
Those who have it know they would be abusing themselves.
Treasure it, learn from it, grow with it and always nurture it.

Celeste Q.

My Cool Breeze

A cool breeze over the mountain
Drifts down to this soul of mine.
It soothes the raging inferno within
And calms me with a strength, sublime.

It's caressing and soothing and gentle
As it brushes across my skin.
I open my window wider
To let more of this cool breeze in.

It soothes as it swirls around me,
Comforting both heart and soul.
It cools as it slowly entwines me
And I surrender to its total control.

The cool breeze over the mountain
Has become a daily routine.
I bask in its gentle feeling
That I long for tho' have never seen.

 Please come to me in the morning,
Soothe me during midday's sun.
Embrace me in the evening
Caress me when the day is done.

Celeste Q.

"One"

Don't paint me like an angel
Then let my feathers singe.
Don't let me crash to the ground
Nor my halo's luster tinge.

Don't colour me in rainbow hues
That fade away with time.
Don't paint me as your sunlight
And expect me to always shine.

Don't put my on a pedestal
From which you know I'll fall.
Don't envision me as a Saint
With my picture on your wall.

But paint me as a woman
The other half of you.
Look at the world through my eyes
The way I look at you.

Look into my mirror
Where only you can see.
The reflection that you see there
Your missing parts are me.

See your imperfections
As only human's flaws
Not a disgrace to hide away
But a pathway and a cause.

Know that I give back to you
The qualities you seek
Missing parts that make you whole
Does not leave me weak.

You give my life a purpose
I - unconditional love.
We complete each other totally
Together we are "one".

Celeste Q.

The Amount I Love You

When I gave you my heart
It was free without impurities.
No malice, no expectations,
No borders or boundaries.
Just a heart, living, breathing,
Laying wide open in your hands.

Cherish it, the only one I have
Or will ever have to give another.
And I give it to you.
The only person that has earned it.
Nurture it. Bath it continuously
In the warmth of your affections.

Feed it love so it can thrive,
Its life depends on you. Know that.
Cradle it gently, it can bruise.
Sing to it, it will keep beat with yours.
Bathe in the warmth it emits.
That warmth is meant only for you.

Don't question its reason or your worth,
That has been predetermined,
It is here in your hands now, you own it.
You control its existence that is faith
In its purest form. That is serious, that
Is enduring. You are what makes my heart live.

Celeste Q.

Gratitude

You freely walked into my life
At a time, I needed you so.
Forgive me if I'm unable
To let my gratitude show.

You stripped me of the necessity
Of my well-formed disguise.
You saw right through my tough veneer
When you looked into my eyes.

You unlocked the chains that stilled my tongue
And forth the hurt did pour.
And though my prattling bothered you
Not once did you close the door.

You held me as I cried for another
You soothed me with your song.
When I needed someone to lean on
You talked with me all night long.

You've seen me at my highest,
Overflowing with gaiety and charm.
You've held me at my lowest,
Your arms were there to keep me warm.

Yes, I am very grateful for you
Though it doesn't always show.
But as you gaze deeply into my eyes
I'm certain that you know.

Celeste Q.

Awakening Souls

Do you see me?
Do you feel me out there?
Can you sense I'm near?
Can you hear my voice whispering in the breeze?
Do you feel the closeness?

Do you see me?
There, way back in the recesses of your mind?
I'm different now, from a different lifetime eons ago.
Do you recognize me still?
Do you search for me in the crowds?

Do you sense me?
Can you sense the change in the air?
The rustling of leaves and birds and the time shift?
Making way to reunite us once again?
Do you sense how close our souls are?

Do you smell me?
When you enter a room am I in the air?
Do you catch a faint whiff of my perfume now and then?
Does the scent of the ocean breeze take you back?
Back to a familiar memory that you can't quite place?

Do you feel me?
The soft thrumming in your chest?
Like feathers floating downward and up together
Enveloping your heart in a warm comforting cloak?
Bringing you feelings of comfort, of innocence, of home?

Do you taste me?
The sea salt ladened air? Where we walked, hand in hand?
Built castles to the skies? Dreaming of our unlived future?
The cotton candy taste long after our last farewell kiss?
Does it still tickle your palate?

Do you yearn for me?
Do you ache at night when your world quiets?
Am I a flicker of memory before your eyes open in the morn?
Are you searching? Longing? Wanting not knowing what?
Is there an unquenchable thirst, hunger, need, emptiness?

Do you remember me?
Back in the age of our first love? Lovers hand in hand
Dancing in the dark. Wishing on the stars.
The warm embraces? The loving glances?
Do your eyes still look for mine?

Do you want me?
Are your long ago promises still fresh in your mind?
Am I still your heart's need and soul's desire?
The one that knew then and does now every part of you?
Is the untamed craving still for me?

I can see you; the veil has thinned.
I can even hear your voice. I can read your thoughts.
I can almost touch you. But I, alas, must wait.
Will you bring me forth into reality, into the light?
Into this lifetime? Will our flames reunite?

Celeste Q.

One True Emotion

Is love a true emotion
Or a reaction to a few?
Is it you I am in love with?
Or my past's reactions
That makes it you?

Love's a combination of many feelings
And I can name you quite a few.
But I can't say for certain if it's love
Or a reaction to you just being you.

Starvation for affection brings
Appreciation for every kiss.
Because of past abuses
Your gentleness I can't resist.

No one appreciated my opinion thus
Your consideration makes me strong.
When others didn't try to really know me
Your needs gave me the feeling I belong.

Having lived a life with lies and deceit
Your honesty refreshes like the rain.
In response to trust placed in me
My respect is what you've gained.

So, is love a true emotion?
Still, I do not know.
Will the combination of feelings
Continue to make it grow?

Will the feelings change and darken?
Will love fade away to hate?
If love is a true emotion
Shouldn't it remain in just one state?

Celeste Q.

Loneliness Of Solitude

Is your life so sullied that you cannot see
The true love knocking at your door?
Are you so scorched from false promises
That your instincts are unreliable anymore?

Can you not decipher reality from dreams?
Are you so confused that you must run and hide?
Can you not appreciate authenticity
When it stands boldly right by your side?

Do you not recognize honest emotions
And separate them from the lies?
Do you not hear the truths in another's word
Nor feel their aching soul as it cries?

Are you trapped in your life of aloneness?
Have you convinced yourself of your strength?
Must you always portray your elevated aura
And justify aloofness at any length?

Can you not own your yearnings and frailties?
Never admit to needing another's warmth?
Must you always be so self-sufficient,
Proclaiming your indifference to another's charm?

Have you never allowed yourself to be vulnerable
In the midst of a passionate night?
Must you always tote your self-reliance?
Does denying loneliness make you feel right?

Do you not crave for a love all encompassing?
Is the truth too hard to admit?
Would your world not shine with a lot more passion
If you welcomed love's warm light within it?

Celeste Q.

No Wishy-Washy Love

I don't want a love that's "ok but..."
I want one that's willing to fight.
Not here one day and then gone away
But one here both morning and night.

I don't want a love that accepts....
I want one that demands.
That endures my emotional storms,
Yet is willing to take both hands.

I don't want a love that allows...
I want one of consistency,
In spite of life's irregularity
That holds me safe in his arms.

I don't want a love that needs...
I want one that sees and accepts
And loves me for just being me,
Is honored to be mine with respect

I don't want a hidden love...
I want one that proclaims.
That the world knows by name
That he's mine - and I his true love.

Celeste Q.

No Words

I want to say "I love you"
In a way never spoken before.
That I need you and I trust you,
Yet the feeling is so much more.

I try to tell you how I feel,
Yet the words ring false-not true.
And I realize the reason is
No words describe how I feel for you.

My love is not of this world
No man was ever given the power,
To capture these feelings with human talents.
No, not in their finest hour.

No canvas could ever portray you,
As you appear to me.
No poem could do you justice,
Something man's incapable to see.

My love is of a heavenly nature.
That one's unable to comprehend.
An infinite feeling that knows no boundaries
No limitations, no beginning, no end.

So don't despair if there's something
I want to say but don't know how,
Although my love is of an infinite nature,
My capabilities are human-here and now.

Celeste Q.

You Are My World

How do I tell you
All that you mean to me?
How can I put into words
The things you cannot see?
You're the dew on the roses,
The leaves on the trees.
The laughter in the hallway,
The fragrance on the breeze.

How do I tell you
So that you'll understand?
How can I make you feel
Like I do when you take my hand?
You're the mountains and the ocean
That make up this land.
You're the glitter of an angel's
Long golden strands.

How do I tell you
So, you'll truly know?
How can words ever show you
That I love you so?
You're the tinkle of fine crystal
The wine's afterglow.
You're the breathtaking beauty,
After new fallen snow.

How do I tell you
So that you can, see?
How to describe the hope
That you've given me?
You're the sparkle of a diamond,
The glow of sunset at sea.
You're all I hold precious.
You're the world to me.

Celeste Q.

Your Gift

I have someone that loves me.
The me I hid inside.
The one I sheltered from the glare
Of others' superficial pride

I thought I'd known love before
In all its glorious ways.
But never did I feel this content
Nor the warmth that it portrays.

The gentle nurturing laughter,
The way it's kissed my soul.
The embrace that's made my heartbeat,
Reaffirming I am whole.

Not fears to run away from but
Encouragement that makes me strong.
The consistent support and affection
That's shown me where I belong.

Celeste Q.

Eternally

Each day I awaken and think of you.
The time that we share is precious.
Every moment is sweet as the morning dew.
Rapture of new love belongs to us.
Never will I stray or even wonder.
All of my being belongs to you.
Let it be known to the heavens up yonder.
Love and life belongs to us two.
Yesterday is tomorrow's memory.

Yours to have as a gift.
Opposed by no other- I'm forever yours.
Upon my heart and last breath, I promise this,
Reap what you wish from my heart and soul.
Sweetheart, my life and love is in your control.

Celeste Q.

The Answer

You ask "Do I love you?"
And, "How do I know?
Will it last forever?"
And "Will our love grow?"

If I knew all the answers
To all your concerns,
I could spare many heartaches
And many fingers once burned.

I'd have wasted no time
Prior to this day.
There would be only you.
In your arms I would stay.

But what could I learn
In such a brief flight through time?
Appreciation and consideration
Would have never been mine.

Gratitude and respect for you
Would have passed right on by.
No gentle longing would radiate
From deep in my eyes.

Do you truly want the answer
At this point of time?
And if it was, "I don't know"
Would you right now be mine?

Or would you pass me right by
In your moment of flight?
To the love of your life
Predetermined to be right.

And then when you touched
Would it be true love you share?
Could you know that for certain?
Not sampling other wares?

Living is a process of learning
Something new every day.
Its past inter-related experiences
That enable me to say
                    "I love you"

Celeste Q.

Time Is Fluid

I've put a lot of miles
Between your heart and mine.
I've picked up the shattered pieces
Of my life and everything's going fine.

Then all at once I see your smile
In the deep recesses of my heart.
And all the work I've spent rebuilding
Is suddenly torn all apart.

I've started life all over,
Now another holds me tight.
I smile and laugh and to all intents
And purposes everything's alright.

Then suddenly you're in my dreams
In the dark hours before dawn.
And this farce that I've been living
Is suddenly all gone.

And I know that I still love you,
You own my heart and soul.
And though I carry on each day
You are always in control.

Because when I see you smile
In the hidden chambers of my mind,
Carrying on this farce is senseless.
My heart's still back with you in time.

Celeste Q.

Don't

Don't read my poems,
Don't get to know me.
Don't speak about love
I'd rather you show me.
Don't promise forever
Lest the sun lose its light.
Don't promise tomorrow
Just live through tonight.

Don't approach me with love
Then take it away.
Don't distance yourself
Yet expect me to stay.
Don't say that you love me
And it's not over,
Then follow it up
With your cold shoulder.

Don't be my lover by day
But a stranger tonight.
Claim all is "OK"
Then disappear out of sight.
Don't tell me you love me
As you distance yourself.
Don't promise to be there
Then leave me in this hell.

Don't pretend to care for me
Then not bother to call.
Don't promise tomorrow
Giving nothing at all.
Don't hand me your tidbits
Of what you call love.
Don't build up my hopes
And then give them a shove.

Don't tell me I scare you
I really don't bite.
Don't blame me for your shyness
Your weakness, or fright.
Don't run hot then cold
I'm still here can't you see?
Let me in all the way
          or
Don't get to know me.

Celeste Q.

Acceptance

When true love is but a shadow,
A dream inside your heart,
A feeling of eternity
Though souls are far apart.

The endless days of searching
In strangers eyes and minds,
The never ending promise
Of the love you pray to find.

The dream that's at your fingertips
But never quite in reach.
That ache that holds you captive
Yet the distance can't be breached.

The longing for completion
That you yearn but never know.
The inability to settle for less
So alone through life you go.

The acceptance of the void
That lives inside your chest
The knowing that no other
Can put your soul to rest.

Celeste Q.

Don't Talk

Just hold me
I don't wanna talk.
Just take me in your arms,
Just rock away my tears.
Hold me all night long,
Wipe away my fears.

I don't want to care,
Nor bear the pain that
Comes from such.
Just hold me in silence
While my heart crumbles.
Know I loved, too damn much.

Celeste Q.

Totality Of My Love

When I say "I love you"
As I gaze into your eyes,
'Tis as though my love encompasses
Each star in the midnight skies.

I see you as a diamond
With many facets shining bright.
Yet all working with each other
To produce the perfect light.

I see you as the oceans
Bringing calmness but also storms.
You are the bitter winter with
A snowy blanket to keep us warm.

I see you as all the elements,
Each disastrous when together.
Yet when viewed alone, yields such life
A beauty unexcelled by any other.

I've seen love in varying degrees
But never could I realize,
My totality of love for every part of you
Shown me free of garnishes and lies.

I see both your good and your bad
Together from which you've grown.
And when I say "I love you",
I mean all of you, As one.

Celeste Q.

Chameleon

I am not like you and am not able to say
Things that deeply affect me as I go through my day.
I express myself this way by playing the clown,
And no one can guess when I'm feeling down.

I laugh and I joke and I play my part well,
And last time I nearly ended it not a soul could tell.
To say "hey, this really hurts me" wouldn't seem quite right
Everyone would shun me and avoid me in fright.

So, I surround myself with laughter and paint on this grin
And I built my suit of armour with many layers of tin.
I've cultivated this reputation, and I've done it so fine.
I compromised myself by choice, was by my own design.

People liked me and accepted me, I'm quite popular this way,
'Til chance delivered a partner who knew me straight away.
He saw my false front for what it had been,
The secrets I shared; he'd already seen.

I show him in poetry the true feelings that I hide.
But he already knows that deep secret side.
I know that I love him way deep in my heart
And I tell him in writing through my form of art.

If it gives him understanding then that's all I could ask,
The poem was a success and well worth the task.

Celeste Q.

My Best Friend

If you could see into my past,
You'd see someone that learned too fast.
The desires of many wrapped all in one.
Yet there's stories to unfold, things still undone.

You'd see someone growing old and grey,
The burdens of life and too little pay.
Someone with a furrowed brow,
The stresses of time worn on me now.

Then along came you, the fountain of youth,
Ridding life's troubles with your boundless truths.
All of my stresses vanished straight away
When you became a part of my every day.

So, ponder yourself naught if I truly love you.
If our love is eternal, if our love will be true.
Whenever in doubt read this poem again.
You will know then my love that you're also
My Only Best friend.

Celeste Q.

Walk With Me

Come walk with me,
Place your hand in mine.
We'll make our own path
Through the sands of time.

We'll smell the blossoms
So tender and fair,
And skirt the mountain sides
With barely a care.

Should storm clouds gather
Over our voyage so fine,
Love will be the cement
That keeps us in line.

We'll shield the raindrops
From each other's eyes.
Then together we'll dream
As the clouds slide by.

True happiness we'll discover
In the dawn's early mist.
Sharing one of love's wonders
As we take time to kiss.

We'll taste nature's beauty
In the smell of the breeze.
Hand in hand we'll dance
Through eternity.

Celeste Q.

My Measurement Of Love

Measure the degree of my Love

Not by the things I say or do

But by my willingness to compromise.

Celeste Q.

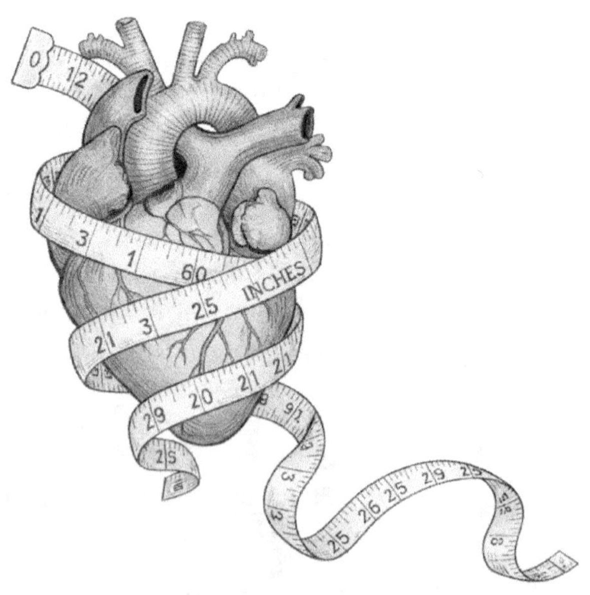

My Love

I look into your eyes and there, dancing off their smile,
Like droplets of a summer rain,
Rejuvenating each tender leaf as you have my life,
I find my dreams.

You smile and it is living proof of existing perfection.
To me you are all, the good, the kind,
The gentle, the wild and the possessor of the only pain
That can truly hurt me.

I am yours, to cherish, to enjoy, to please, to destroy.
I have given you my heart and life as one.
The greatest compliment, treat it with gentleness and respect.
It is a life.

You stand before me so proud, every hope, dream, wish of my life
Encaptured in your being.
My search through eternity has now ended. It is you.
At last, we have touched.

The magical moment of ensnarement is here, and yet,
With great sorrow I gaze upon you.
For I see only a man, with likes, dislikes and ambitions.
And I, a woman, the slave of life's unfairness.

So, take back your life, go bear your fruits and find your answers,
For I have lived too soon, and my fruits have ripened.
Go quickly my love, and in your heart take my life.
I pray it sees you through a safe journey.

Celeste Q.

The Word Commitment

I heard the word commitment
Whispered in my ear.
Though spoken oh so softly,
The meaning was crystal clear.

It opens up a whole new world,
One I'd never known.
Having someone to care for me,
Never needing to face life alone.

It lends a shoulder, broad and strong
To support me in my hardest time.
An arm to cuddle me through the night
'Til the morning sun begins to shine.

Ten fingers came along with the word
And two hands so gentle and strong.
A chest so warm and comforting,
And a smile when I'm feeling down.

"Good morning, babe" to start my day,
Fills the void of waking alone.
Someone to walk close by my side,
No more dinners for two, on my own.

Promises of someone to rely on,
A love with no reservations or fear.
There once was a time this word scared me,
But it now has a meaning so dear.

Celeste Q.

I Cherish You

How do I begin to thankyou
For all you've given me?
Dreams of a future and belonging,
All the things that you can't see.

Hopes again are in my heart
Where emptiness once had lived.
A prayer and some ambition,
These things to me you give

Now never mind the cost my dear.
It's not too high to pay.
Some silly tears splashed on my pillow,
A small price for my todays.

Don't dwell on what you've done to me
Nor the tears you've made me cry.
It's all the things you've given me,
My life, I'd been denied.

These are the things I'm thankful for
As by your side I stay.
I cherish you completely
And give thanks for you each day.

Celeste Q.

Parallel Worlds

We've traveled our parallel worlds apart
Lonely, and always questioning why?
The unfairness of life, heavy on our hearts
Wondering why happiness brushed us by.

So many dreary years alone and lost
Yet driven by unseen forces to go on.
Wanting to give up - the towel to toss.
Still questioning "Why?" when the race we'd won.

Now here we are together, our worlds now one.
Our "Whys" are now answered for us at last.
Understanding fills our hearts. Lets in the sun.
The weary years alone are now in the past.

Life was not being unfair to us we now see,
The burdens were there for us to learn from.
The path a preparation for our life that would be
To learn from and appreciate from now on.

We bend now where once we wouldn't budge,
We have learned well how lonely "One" truly is.
We accept where at one time we would have judged.
Our pasts have taught us well our weaknesses

Our parallel worlds weren't so far apart,
They were always traveling toward each other's.
We were just being well prepared for the part
Of spending eternity together as lovers.

Celeste Q.

Familiar Love

I stretch forth my hand
And my fingertips brush your cheeks.
'Tis as though the very wonderment of life
Lies there just below the surface.
A placid pool of secrets patiently waiting
For me to ripple it's mirror like surface.

My fingertips touch, then pass through
And the warmth of your love bathes my hand.
Forever swirling, weaving its ways under my skin.
Till my very body becomes its conductor
The life's source on which these secrets nurture.
And thus, through this mutual parasitic need
I know life, as a babe it's mother.

As one self-sufficient entity
We feed upon and nurture each other
In one continuous recycling motion.
The constant reaction breeds familiarity,
Insuring the new to soon become an old entrusted friend.
Through this subconscious intermingling I know you.
For now, we are joined, one union, one entity, one life.

Celeste Q.

I Look For You

When you're gone
I look for you.
When I'm in a crowded place
I look for you.
When I'm down and need a smile
I look for you.
When I just need a hug
I look for you.
When I need sunshine in my day
I look for you.
For so many years now
I look for you.
And at last, you're here and
I'll always look only for you.

Celeste Q.

Falling

Poetry and palpitations running through my mind.
The tingling deep down to my toes is beating out the time.
The quivering of my eyelids and the shaking of my hands,
Is something all brand new to me, that I don't understand?

Something's taken up the space where my mind once had control.
It has stolen my heart and senses and is coming for my soul!
There doesn't seem to be a way that I could ever stop
Outside influences hitting hard and landing out on top.

To fight the fight would be in vain and nothing would, I win.
The palpitations start again, now making my head spin.
How to regain composure and come out looking cool
When just one glance melts the ice -and I, a blubbering fool.

What is this thing that's lorded over every part of me?
Please someone help, I have no strength to halt it don't you see?
Oh, tell me lord what's happening? I pray to him above.
You silly girl, don't you know? You've fallen deep in love.

Celeste Q.

It Is Meant To Be

Will you always be there?
My darling asks of me.
How can I answer his questions,
In a way that he might see?

Why do the birds fly freely,
Yet animals walk the ground?
Why do the stars flare brightly,
Before they plummet down?

Why do the mountains stand so tall,
Rugged yet so majestically?
What is it that puts the sparkle,
On even the smallest sea?

How many sands in the desert?
Why can I not see a sound?
Why is the earth not flat like a map?
But nearly perfectly round?

There's so many unsolved questions
Whose answers are still a mystery.
God made everything for his reason
Just accept it was meant to be.

Celeste Q.

Questions

You've always been inside my heart.
I've known you all along,
And yet with such bewilderment
I wonder why you've come.

You show me how you love me,
And still, I question "why?"
I have so many faults you see.
The main one, how do I try?

How to make your love grow,
To stay inside your heart?
To keep you happy, fulfill your needs
To live up to my part.

Wanting this does scare me,
I'm only me you know.
Just a woman with no pedestal
I've nothing else to show.

Do not be disappointed
When you see me as I am.
No feathered wings are on this angel,
But I'd be proud to take your hand.

Celeste Q.

Category 4

Heartbreak

Dear God

My heart is so heavy with this pain called life.
The thoughts of a tomorrow cut like a knife!
Slicing me deep into my soul.
Leaving me isolated without control.

The tears never ending burning my skin.
The hurt I let out but the torture stays in.
The guilt, always pushing, being my guide.
A significant approval still being denied.

The strength of my being is fast fading away,
I doubt I can survive through one more day.
God lessen this load and give me a path.
I'm lost and alone and I feel your wrath.

I've lived it each day, not knowing why?
I've given my all and still I do try.
Please help me and tell me, what should I do?
Please guide me and show me how to get through.

This darkness, despair, unknown night of my soul.
I'm paralyzed, I can't breathe, I have no control.
You have plunged me into this hell, I can't fight.
Please show me a path forward, please lend me some light.

Please steel my heart to do as I must.
Please soften my will to give you, my trust.
Please show me the rainbow across the bridge.
Please give me the strength to climb this last ridge.

Amen

Celeste Q.

Dream's Bite

Today I kiss my dreams goodbye.
I put them in a golden box.
One that will keep them sealed tight
With a sturdy keyless lock.

They'll never come back to haunt me
Nor leak out piece by piece.
I'll not partake of the agony
The memories will cease.

My heart is much too tender
To bear the pain of loss.
My years are far too many
To waste on groundless cause.

My soul is far too withered
From unawakened dreams.
My days are far too numbered
To fulfill with futile means.

My tears will salt the contents,
Preserving them inside.
My heart will go on beating
Though my future's been denied.

The box will keep its shine aglow
It will be my guiding light.
If ever I dare to dream again,
It will remind me of love's bite.

Celeste Q.

This Last Teardrop

This tear clings to my lash
Hovering just above strength
And total emotional chaos.

Undecided, do I fall for my own
pain,
For the pain of ever losing you?
Or the pain of the world?

Because my heart right now
Feels enough for the world.
And it must count, it is my last
tear.

I eliminate me for tho' lonely, I
will survive.
I ponder over you in great
concern.
Alas, I know another will hold
you dear.

As I let this last teardrop fall, I
know,
It cries for all the pain in the
world.
Yes, for the world's pain and
suffering

I let this last teardrop fall,
For even the sun is too far to hug the world.

Celeste Q.

Pieces of Me

Today I ripped my heart out,
I tore it from my soul.
I chewed and clawed and scratched
at it
Until I gained control.

My heart said "don't be stupid."
My soul said "this ain't right."
My mind said "just get rid of him-
Put him out of sight."

So today I tore my heart out
It's lying bleeding in a heap.
I thought that it would break the
spell
That's causing me to weep.

My heart screamed "put me back
again"
My soul whispered "I can't breath"
My mind said "I told you he was
lying"
When he said he wouldn't leave."

But I can't put back the pieces.
They're laying mangled on the floor.
So, I'm trapped here with this mind of mine,
Alone forevermore.

Celeste Q.

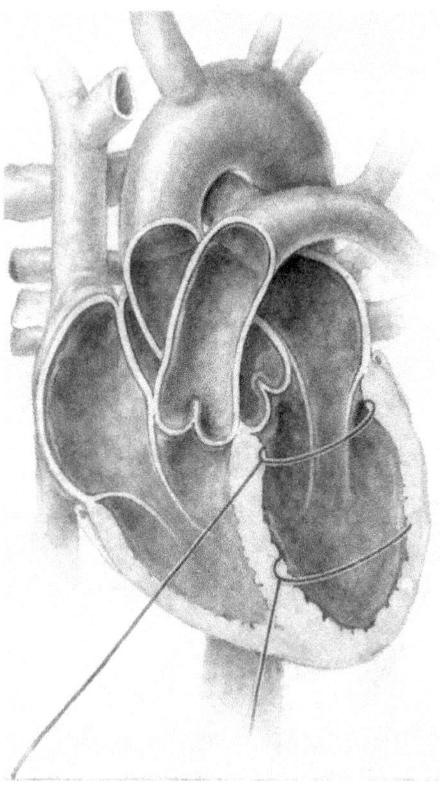

Putting Back The Pieces

I picked my heart up from the heap where it lay,
And pinned it back to my soul.
For it was obvious to me, straight away
That the mind should not have control.

It will take you down corridors where you will be lost
And pathways so dreary and dark.
It will block out the sunlight and drain all the colour
And leave your world barren and stark.

The soul couldn't run things, it barely could breathe,
To contain one's spirit was why it was conceived.
"Not my job", it exclaimed when I asked it to work.
"I couldn't begin to control that Jerk!"

I asked my mind "Would you mind stepping down?"
It laughed at me, said "Ha! You think I'm a clown!"
You gave me this power and now it is mine"
And I think I run things perfectly fine!"

With great trepidation I looked at my heart.
Lying there in its heap, not likely to start.
But I patched it together as best as I could
And prayed it would work for all of our good.

It started to pump with its rhythm so pure.
I was back on track, of that, I was sure.
My soul let out a sigh, a comforting sound.
One I wanted forever to please stay around.

I looked for my mind, but I couldn't see
It was hiding up there away from me.
Sulking in silence from its fast demotion,
Hating the competition and commotion.

All working together as so it should be,
Not one in control, but a group of all three.
My mind was outnumbered, it couldn't compete.
It knew right away that I was complete.

Celeste Q.

Doing Time

Break all the clocks my wait is done.
My heart lies empty, my soul is gone.
Days run into tomorrow's.
Alone I'll be.
Break the clocks, release the pain.
Set this tormented mind free.
Release the chains that time has bound.
Let me drift to the new life I've found.
Fast forward the time
To meet my fate.
Drop the chains, release the servitude.
Stop this endless cycle of hate.
Tear up the contracts of an emotional past.
Relinquish my debt, set me free at last.
Let me live my life,
My mistakes.
Stand aside, let me go, clear my path.
Wish me strength for what it takes.

Celeste Q.

Before You

I found my happy space and lived it well before you.
Then suddenly an uninvited light entered my world.
A glow so warm and comforting
That I peeled off the layers to feel
Your warmth within my soul.

I basked in the heat your light emitted.
So calm, so consistent, that I forgot to keep a layer on.
Then slowly I felt a chill, a little one,
Creeping in, barely detectable yet there.
And I was forced to put my first layer back on.

But day after day I still felt warmth in the glow.
Slowly it got chilly again and another layer went on.
And again, I felt comfort. Then chilled,
Then another layer, more comfort, more chill...
And so, it repeated and so I retreated.

Now I have put back all the layers, I've covered myself
I've hidden my flesh, my feelings, my soul.
But I yearn for that comforting glow.
The one that saw me, unashamed and naked.
The calm inviting warmth that permeated me.

Now I'm here again in my own space like before you.
But locked in, under layer upon layer upon extra layers.
Yet I feel no comfort, no heat, no light.
No consistent warmth, just a chill.
And again tho' I'm here in my own space, there is no happy.

Celeste Q.

The Reality Slap

It's better to have loved and lost
Said no one that ever paid the cost.
'Tis better far to have avoided it all
Than accepting you've been tossed.

The ego snaps, the pride is gone.
The heart is cracking and you're alone.
And this is better? Said no one!
What's better is, if it's left undone.

Don't go there in the first place.
Back out with dignity and grace.
Cement those blocks, build high the wall,
Stop your pride from having to crawl.

Regain your composure, show your strength.
Avoid this hell at any length.
Take back your power and your pride.
Stop the trust-open eyes wide.

Start looking at what you really see,
Not at what you want it to be.
Accept the obvious for what it is
Don't make excuses nor dismiss.

If they say love though you're never together
Prepare yourself for stormy weather.
Watch the flags along the way
They will not lead your heart astray.

It's better to have loved? A lie.
Spoken by those that didn't try.
At least no one that's worn these shoes
Or ever had to pay my dues.

Celeste Q.

The Path

Don't go down that path.
You did that once before.
You barely came out with your life
And you vowed to nevermore.

Don't go down that path
Though the flowers there are sweet.
The nectar and the fruit are such
That nothing can compete.

Don't go down that path.
It will break your heart in two.
It'll chew you up and spit you out
And there's nothing you can do.

Don't go down that path.
I've warned you pay me heed.
You've lived this long all by yourself
And managed to succeed.

Don't go down that path.
Love wasn't meant for you.
You're a clam that can't be opened
Without breaking you in two.

Don't go down that path.
It's misery and despair.
There's only tears and heartbreak
Waiting for you there.
Don't go down that path.

Celeste Q.

Lessons Untold

I used to walk on the clouds so high,
Could touch the eternal light in the sky.
A twinkling star would cover me with its shining rays
And I would lavish in the Milky Way.

Then a thunderbolt struck with great dismay
Plunging my cloud on a new and tenous way.
The pulsating rains stung and splashed my face.
Torrents of rain came from an unknown place.

The eternal light is love you see
It can blacken the soul for eternity.
When used with no remorse or regret
It can make the mind never forget.

The lightening bolt is a razor-sharp knife
It pierces the soul while letting in strife.
The rain that cuts and slashes your face
Is a deadly viper striking in an unknown place.

Clouds of joy will slowly dissipate
Shrunken by the torrents of anger and hate.
The Arc left behind by the sun and the rain
Is there to remind you of the horrendous pain.

So, if you should walk on clouds so high
And you happen to see a lone star go by,
Remember that it could soon turn into rain.
Should one fleeting star cause so much pain?

Celeste Q.

Love's Pain

The pain won't hurt much, it will subside
The pain is killing, they must have lied.
It's never ending, constantly pounding
Tears are flowing, I am drowning!

The pain won't hurt much, don't believe.
It's never ending- there's no reprieve.
With every glimpse it rears again
From this new pain I can't refrain.

The pain won't hurt much, it's killing me!
It shreds my heart-won't set it free.
It lifts my spirits high, then, a flash
It's back to earth in another crash.

This pain won't hurt much I was told
Just cherish it like finest gold.
Don't try to run, don't try to hide
Don't think you'll escape its clutch alive.

This pain won't hurt much, 'til too late
And you've become the final bait
To twist and turn and toy and play.
Then without a care just toss away.

Celeste Q.

The Hurt Within

If you're searching for answers
Look deep in my eyes.
Down into their depths
Where my memories lie.

If you still cannot find them
Don't quit in despair.
Look past the tears to that void
When you were not there.

Perhaps I appear to be
In total control.
It's not surface damage but
Deeper, down in my soul.

Like an apple that shines
With a rub and some spit,
Deep within there's a rot
Caused by one bad pit.

I've lived through too much
For lies and deceit.
I hide my heart well
Yet still my heart weeps.

The damage to my faith
Has left a large tear,
Yet with reassurance and time
It will completely repair.

Celeste Q.

Disinfecting Love

I've wiped my own last tear.
I've wiped the last drop of blood
That oozed from this broken heart.
I've wiped you from my page of life.

I've erased all traces of our past.
I've dumped my feelings with the trash
Where they were always meant to be.
I've taken back all promises made .

I've read the self-help journals.
I've learned to put my feelings first,
Where they should have been all along.
I've erased the songs from my devices.

I've self-hypnotized to forget you.
I've self-medicated so not to feel you,
Which just about made me puke.
I've survived four waking hours without you.

I've spent the day doing the work.
I've checked and rechecked the list
Wondering if there's anything I've missed.
I've yet to figure out that elusive feeling.

I've re-examined every little thing I thought of.
I've disinfected my whole world,
Which has been sorely neglected and yet
I've just realized I'm still too deep in love.

Celeste Q.

The Fool

I played your game
From page to page.
I chased in unrelentless rage.
I questioned why you came along
I cherished your love, my heart's song.

I felt the growth within my soul.
I smiled as I lost all control.
I played and joked and smiled away,
Never intending to betray
The person that I was.

I trusted that although a game,
If I bared my all you'd know my name.
That I could find a love deep and true
And turn this game around on you.
But I was so very wrong.

My will is no match for you
I am not that cold, calloused ,cruel.
When I say love, I love for real.
When I trust, it's in the truth I feel.
But not you, my love.

I wasn't one of 15000 others,
All dreaming that they are your lovers.
No, I'm fifteen thousand and one
And what a silly fool I've become.
Just another, I meant nothing to you.

I went through changes in my life,
I am now alone, no one's wife.
Wasted time I should have spent.
My world is lost, totally rent.
In solitude I ask "where are you?"

Celeste Q.

Still I Stayed

I buried myself,
I found my safe space
And there I stayed.
Long after the show had played out,
After the birds had flown,
And the snows had melted.
Still I Stayed.
I thought of leaving, but for what?
Nothing out there. This soul was empty.
No desire to try no need, to accumulate
Stuff and memories and feelings.
I knew time was passing,
But still I stayed.
I watched the world from here
In my safe cocoon. Always turning,
An unending turning without purpose,
Without emotions, hate or love.
A void, a safe void in a safe space.
Waiting, hurrying the passage to a new life.
But still I stayed.
Then you arrived and time no longer
Was the enemy. Now, I needed more.
I'd wasted mine in my safe space.
You brought love, I needed like a sponge.
I bathed in it, soaked in it, languished in it
Like tomorrow would never come.
Believing you'd always stay-need my love.
Then you beckoned me, coaxed me, cajoled me.
Tried to have me join you but I couldn't.
Though my heart was breaking, my life ending,
I just couldn't. I said goodbye.
I was forever shackled to my safe space.

Celeste Q.

Just Play

I don't want to talk to you.
Not your business what's my name.
If I'm married or I'm single
Doesn't matter, not my game.

Where I live or what country?
Is of no interest to me.
I'm just here to play the game
And not a target will I be.

If you want someone to talk to,
Better find a different source.
Been there - already did that
And let nature run its course.

Now I'm back here where I started.
Just trying to play the game.
And I don't want to talk.

Celeste Q.

Broken Tea Cup

I'm dying here, I've given up
There are no tea leaves in my cup.
My future's broken, gone is my past.
Along with the present, they didn't last.

I've fought the fight for twenty years,
I cried alone and hid my tears.
One tiny candle in the dark
Kept me alive within its spark.

I always kept my soul intact,
Kidding myself that I would fight back.
That I'd use those gifts God gave to me
And they would help to break me free.

That I'd find the love that I deserved,
Yet here am I still undisturbed.
My true love waits so patiently
For the person I cannot let him see.

The joys we shared were my last.
And time is wasting, going fast.
There is no future here with me
There is no more, I'm defeated.

Take a look. See what you'll see.
There's nothing really left of me.
I honestly thought that I could
Love you back, the way I should.
But unfortunately, I am broken.

Celeste Q.

Category 5

Depression

I Pray

Cool down this hell, that I might breathe,
For this dear Lord I pray.
Swing open a window that I might see,
The light of but one more day.
Bring forth a bed and let me lie
To rest these weary bones.
A pillow to cushion this ladened heart.
That weighs heavy as any stone.

Lend me your hand to lighten this load,
And a smile upon your face.
That I might find the strength I need
In your warm embrace.
A word of praise to give me hope
When all my own has gone.
One tiny candle to shine my path.
That I might carry on.

Celeste Q.

Inner Strength

Yesterday I prayed.
No one heard so
I prayed louder.
Still no one heard
So I cried harder.

When tears ran dry
I heard.
I heard what I'd
Prayed for.

Strength,

My prayers were heard
By myself.
I found the strength
To get through the hell.
To wake up and face
One more day.

Celeste Q.

When You Cry

When you're so damn mad that you've trapped yourself so far inside.
That even tho' you're suffocating, even tho' you're drowning in your
pain,
You can't climb out of the pit.
You can't break free of the chains.

When you're so damn hurt because you've trapped yourself so deep
inside
That you just lean back and watch as your love and life passes you by.
You can't reach out for their help.
You can't allow them to try.

When you're so damn alienated and you've trapped yourself in your dark.
And you know you'll always be the outsider looking into someone else's
light.
Never to bring its glow into your life.
Never to allow your heart to take flight.

When you're so damn scared that you will spend forever alone in this pit.
You can't chance not grabbing the brass ring, not hanging on for dear
life.
Never letting go of this chance
Never giving up on this love.

When you're so damn scared to love but even more scared to let it go.
That's when you cry.

Celeste Q.

Childhood Dreams

When I was a little girl
I had so many big dreams.
I'd be rich and famous and well loved,
Oh yes, I had those dreams.

They kept me company as a child,
My friends in times of stress.
When no one else could be bothered
I wore them like a dress.

When Mother yelled and Father drank
My dreams kept me company.
I held my head high so determined
My dreams were all I'd ever need.

As life forced me to grow up
My dreams fell by the way.
I knew with each one's passing
I'd be all alone one day.

Now I cannot hold my head high,
My determination is all gone.
I'll never be that little girl again.
I've no dreams to keep me strong.

So here I stand on my own now.
No dreams to keep me company.
When someone yells, another drinks
I've only tears to comfort me.

Celeste Q.

Depression

Reflections on the water
Of such a desperate face.
Ripples fading repeatedly,
Yet tears they've not erased.

Confusion of existence,
Life's web of lies still weaves.
Your cross becomes so heavy
'Til every emotion bleeds.

But look into the waters,
Don't let it be your bed.
For when you're at your low tide
A high tide lies ahead.

Reach into the depth of your soul,
Hang onto just one smile.
Depression is a healing.
I know I've walked that mile.

Celeste Q.

A Better Life

When life crashes down in a horrendous rage
And you wake up having lived ten times your age,
Turn the page.

Open a blank page and write it anew.
Rewrite it with laughter, erase and re-do.
Turn the page.

When the heavens crack open and you fear you will drown,
Hang onto your sanity as you climb to higher ground.
Turn the page.

Rewrite it with rainbows, sunshine and dreams.
The page is yours to write with whatever it seems.
Turn the page.

Rewrite each chapter one page at a time.
Choosing to cautiously replace every line.
Turn the page.

When your chapters are finished and you've written each line
Life's end is nearing, you think, but while there's still time
Start again...
Turn the page.

Celeste Q.

The Longest Day

Today, the longest day.
The day you bare your soul.
The day you lay your past present and future in
The hands of your lover.
The day you say, here I am, this is me,
The inside and out.
The day you say take me as I am or toss me.
The day you realize your love is too deep to hide.
The day all games and secrets must end.
The day you know love.
The day you realize you've reached your destiny.
The day you know your very soul is in his hands.
The day you wait for your lover's final decision.
The longest day.

Celeste Q.

Secret Strength

When your darkness creeps to the forefront
And a stranger wears your skin.
When the goodness has forsaken you
And the devil flashes your grin.

When you hide behind your demons
Begging to be set free.
Though you learned to hide it well
There's one who truly sees.

They hold you in the sunlight
When all is easy and soft.
But they cherish you in your darkness
When you're feeling all is lost.

The demons that haunt you, they've slain
In their time before You came.
No threat is Satan to their strength
Or the powers they have gained.

Trust them to be there to hold you
In the stillness before dawn.
Believe in the magical healing powers
Their strength is for you to lean on.

Your healing is all that's desired
Bringing comfort in your darkest nights
Your safety as you tread hell's waters
'Til your back to your world's best light.

Celeste Q.

Resilience

Don't die today.
Let loose the tears,
Let them fly.
Do whatever it takes,
But just don't die.

Break open your heart
Toss away the pieces.
Shed all the pain.
Let them lie where they fall.
Your loss will be your gain.

Struggle through the day,
Hold on for the night.
Hell's that place in your mind.
Feelings and memories allowed
Are taking you back to that time.

Hurts and self-hate you've allowed
Creep to the forefront, feel them now.
Like a new scar, a wound,
A huge gaping hole
From which there's no escape.
You've lost total control.

But not today....

Today I won't die.
I let loose the pain and yes, I'll cry.
I'll feel the guilt and carry on,
I'll mourn the loss of all that's gone.
Yes, I hate this thing called life,
But today I won't die.

Celeste Q.

Panic

Panic Attacks
What is that?
It's when you exhale much deeper and
Slower than you inhale.

It's when arrows are coming at you
From all possible directions.
And your arms and hands bleed from
Trying to thwart them, to protect your inner world.

And you're just too tired to continue,
So, you lay down in complete exhaustion
And just exhale.

Celeste Q.

Don't Want To Be

Loved any more
To hurt any more
To be happy any more
To be sad anymore

To be alone any more
To be in a crowd anymore
To try any more
To give up any more

To cry anymore
To laugh any more
To write any more
To fight any more

To work anymore
To sleep any more
To sing any more
To dance any more

To smile any more
To joke any more
To survive any more
To be anymore

Celeste Q.

Can You Shake It?

When depression comes and takes control
Of the deepest darkest corners of your soul
Can you make it through? You just don't know.
Can you take it?
Can you fake it?
Can you shake it?
Can you make it?
You...... just ...... don't...... know.

When your light grows dim and you're all alone
Will you get through the darkness on your own?
Will you see a new day? You just don't know.
Can you make it?
Can you shake it?
Can you break it?
Can you take it?
You...... just...... don't ...... know.

When the deepest night transcends your soul
And your world is cycling without control
Will the sun ever shine? You just don't know.
Can you shake it?
Can you fake it?
Can you break it?
Can you take it?
Can you make it?
You...... just ...... don't...... know.

Celeste Q.

Category 6

Love in 5D

Lord Of The Universe

Please know that I've never met them
But my love is deep and real.
Please guide them to my inner world
And show them how I feel.

Give them knowledge to trust their feelings
And strength to accept this love.
Although we've never crossed paths in life
This was destiny gifted from above.

I do not love their human form
Nor their worldly wealth or place.
The ties that bind are much deeper,
Ones that time will not erase.

I love the core of their inner self
Their inner strengths and beliefs.
Our souls intertwine like the densest vine,
Tightly woven, unable to release.

Let me be the companion of their soul
The truest friend to all they're needs.
Let them accept this token of love freely
Let it bring them comfort and peace.

Amen

Celeste Q.

Is it Me You're Looking For?

Hello, this is love knocking at your door.
I'm here to meet you, please let me in,
I don't want to be a stranger anymore.

I've felt your energies pulling me
For quite some time it seems.
I tried to meet you often in your nightly dreams.

I rapped upon your subconscience
But no reply was there.
Now I knock at your heart's door in utter despair.

I need to get to know you, to show you how I feel.
I'm not just a passing daydream.
I'm still here my love, and I'm real.

I'm all that has been missing in your daily life,
To shoulder your pain and sorrow
And help guide you through your strife.

Hello this is love I'm waiting here once more.
Please open up and greet me.
Let in me in and unlock your door.

Celeste Q.

You're my Candle

In this vast world I flew
Clueless without plans.
Avoiding any obstacles
Shunning life's demands.

You entered unannounced,
I noticed you were there.
Yet still I flew endlessly
Without a single care.

Then you lit your candle
And I came closer to take a look.
I couldn't resist the wavering glow
And in your warmth I shook.

I tried to pull back from you
But all the paths seemed bare.
I kept returning continuously
Praying you were there.

Your candle lit my heart and soul.
It guided me on my flight.
I flew to you with no control
Addicted to your light.

So here I flutter nightly
I have no one else to blame.
I can't resist your flickering light
I 'm but a moth to your flame.

Celeste Q.

Love In 5D

Welcome to the new world
Proclaims an old soul from the past.
It's nice to view the world again
And see that some things last.

But what's this new way of meeting?
And how are you to know
That the internet will guide your heart
To where it needs to go?

You can send them hearts and flowers
Smiles and hugs and waves.
But are these internet kisses
What your modern hearts really crave?

What happened to the old ways?
Like dinners and dates and shows.
Who are you even talking to?
Does anyone really know?

Please tell me how one does this?
I do really need to know
What to send if I get stood up.
Or where do all the broken hearts go?

And if the romance withers
And your love goes cold or flees,
Please tell me is it acceptable
To send him several poop emojis?

Not that I need to do this
My online love is doing fine.
But I need to know what emojis do what
So, the poop doesn't mix with the wine.

Celeste Q.

Online Love

Take me far away, if only in my mind
Share with me a little while, a gentler bit of time.
Lead me through your life's journeys
And I'll slowly show you mine.
Take me around the world with you,
If only in my mind.

Walk with me along the mythical shores
And reach up to the midnight stars.
Pick a bouquet of them for me
To brighten my darkest hours.
Then dance with me til midnight,
If only in my mind.

Whisper lover's words to me, if only in my mind.
Hold me till the new dawn awakens,
And let me pretend that you are mine.
Then smile and click, send me on my way.
And I will cherish our precious time.
If only in my mind.

Celeste Q.

The Tablet

You tugged on my heart strings,
I shoved you back on the shelf.
You tugged a little harder,
I unplugged you - loved myself.

You sent another emoji,
I pushed you further away.
You sent me a beautiful soul,
Now I'm trapped here another day.

You blinked and you buzzed
And you pinged every day,
'Til I opened you back up
And finally begged you to stay.

I grabbed my pen and paper
Writing fiercely of love.
But you'd relinquished my heart
When I gave that last shove.

I dusted off my tablet and
Recharged it each night.
Hoping beyond reason
That I'd again see your light.

But too long I've waited in vain
It's no longer blinking for me
And now I question myself.
Was this even reality?

Celeste Q.

Fading

You spoke about love dangled like a carrot
And I gobbled it up like a sponge.
You offered eternity
I thought I could share it.
Visions of where we belong.

You winked and I hugged offered flowers -I love
And two months were gone in a flash.
My face was all smiles,
Our chats ran for miles
Not expecting this online to last.

Days into weeks, weeks into months
Across the miles our hearts soared
We smiled and we hugged,
We kissed and we waved
Love grew daily, no longer bored.

Four months have now gone and I'm still all alone.
And I question when will reality set in?
We chat everyday but I don't see a way
For our futures to ever begin.

The vibes are much lower the chats coming slower
The hugs and the kisses all but gone.
You no longer wave, now you don't seem to crave
And I wonder if your love has moved on.

Celeste Q.

Emoji Love Poem

I 🖤 u my 😊 🖤 the 👤 said.
I'll 🖤 u 4evr til I am dead.
The 👤 😄d 😊 ly + tilted her head
Dreaming of the ✦ day they were wed.

There were white 🕊s and 🌹 🌹
And fine 🍷 🍷 galore
There were 🍰 🥞 of all types
And 🐕 friends for sure.

The ☀ shone so ☀ on their day
Even the ☁ ⛅ 🏃 far away.
The 🍃 🖤 ly ♪♫ thrilled from the 🌲 🎄.
The 🐛 🐞 crawled away as did the 🐝 🐝 🐝.

Twas a match made in heaven 😊
And it is to this day.
But heaven 😊 🚫
Should emojis go away!

Emoji Love Poem

I love you my sweetheart, the man said.
I'll love you forever, 'til I am dead.
The lady smiled sweetly and tilted her head.
Dreaming of the day they were wed.

There were white doves and roses
And fine wine galore
There were cakes of all types
And best friends for sure.

The sun shone so bright on their day
Even the clouds ran far away.
The birds' lovely music thrilled from the trees.
The bugs crawled away as did the bees.

'Twas a match made in heaven,
And it is to this day.
But heaven forbid
Should emojis go away!

Celeste Q.

New Start

I'm looking to see if you're looking at me
To apologize would make things worse.
So, my distance I take
Hoping the break
Will lessen the pain of my curse.

My smile is gone, replaced with a frown.
No hugs, no kisses, no heart.
They all went away,
You took them that day,
When you took it on yourself to depart.

I check my blank screen, hoping I'm unseen.
Where all my dreams of you live.
Still nothing is there,
But total despair,
Because neither is willing to give.

So, I drop a hug and a kiss and a prayer
A feeble attempt at a new start.
Hoping you just can't resist
That one great big kiss.
And it opens the door to your heart.

Now I'm looking to see if you're looking at me.
To apologize would be a new start.
So, I'm sorry my love,
Here's a 💋 and a 🎁,
And I 🙏 that you send back your ❤️.

Celeste Q.

You're There.

Where? Everywhere.
You're in my alarm clock when I wake up.
That first glimpse of the day.

You're in my coffee cup, that first bold sip.
You're in my messages when I check.
To see what you had to say.

You're in my mind when I drive my car.
When I take a wrong turn its because
You were there.

You're in my dinner as I go to eat,
By the way, avocados aren't too sweet.
They're very bland.

You're in my poetry that I try to write.
And I'm sure you'll be in my dreams
Again tonight.

Celeste Q.

Good Morning Babygirl

"Good morning babygirl" is all it takes to brighten up my day.
A simple smile of acknowledgement when you are on your way.
A heart to know you hear me, a gentle hug at night.
A smile and a kiss and everything's alright.

Loving at a distance can be difficult they say,
But all it takes is just a wave to brighten up the day.
Just knowing that you're out there and that you really care
Has made my life much easier, and all the pains I bear.

A gentle hug and sweet kiss puts a smile on my face.
The love I found on my blue screen cannot be replaced.
I look for it each morning and embrace it every night.
It's my final thought and feeling before I shut the light.

Loving you has been easy, such a natural thing.
Your love and understanding has made my aching heart sing.
My mind has been seduced, my soul laid open and bare.
Your baby girl lies waiting for the love she hopes to share.

Celeste Q.

Where?

Where does my love go when I give it away?
Once it leaves my body.
When you're here with me then I can surely say,
When you're not, where does my love go?

Does it find you in the crowds?
Or does it just flow freely out in space?
For I know I'm still giving, it's still flowing.
But where does my love go when I give it away?

Do you still feel it where you are?
Does it warm your heart and soul?
Can you even tell that I'm still giving?
You my love with no control?

Will it come back to me as it always does?
I have no way to know.
Will it miss your heart and fall short
And fizzle at my feet?

Tell me where does my love go when I give it away?

Celeste Q.

Just Wishful Thinking

Just tell yourself he wasn't real.
Convince yourself that you don't feel
The tearing pain deep in your soul
So close to losing all control.

Convince yourself it wasn't you.
There was nothing else that you could do.
Pretend your fine and you will grow.
A learning curve and nothing more.

Just tell yourself it wasn't meant to be,
That you are glad He set you free.
You didn't like his gentle ways,
His smile that brightened up your day.

His smiling emojis so cute and bright.
The change in your world, so much light.
The comfort of home that both of you shared.
Your stupidity thinking, he really cared.

Just tell yourself reality is by far
Better than dreaming on any star.
Toss your tablet back on its shelf.
Relax, rewind, convince yourself.

Celeste Q.

Today I Say Goodbye.

Goodbye old world, you've served me well.
The lessons learned in my heart will dwell.
Goodbye the old material things,
Letting you go for what new life brings.

Goodbye old morals and traditional times
I've now outgrown those ties that bind.
Goodbye the emotions of a time before
You can't come with, through tomorrow's door.

Goodbye the memories and the pain,
But thank you for your gifts I've gained.
Goodbye my friends for all these years.
Your love is something I'll forever hold dear.

Goodbye to me that once I was.
I had to outgrow you, the time has come.
Release the old - to the winds let it fly.
Waiting for the "Today" when I say Goodbye.

Celeste Q.

When The Muse Is Amused

You came to me with words of gold
And a smile lights up my face.
I tried to discover who you were
But alas there was no trace.

We talked for days then weeks and months
And still it wasn't clear.
Although you were but a fantasy,
Still, I held you dear.

Slowly as the time did pass,
I noticed an unusual thing.
So many online videos and memes
Had such a familiar ring.

I started feeding messages
In ways that it would show.
And sure, enough my words came back
As if I would not know.

But all the time he used my trust
And even though I seethed,
I had to admit to myself
I had motives up my sleeve.

His many videos would quickly pass,
Forgotten by the mind.
While my book of poems he gave, would grow
And gain followers over time.

(Thank You ☺)

Celeste Q.

About the Author

Celeste Quackenbush was born, raised, and lives in Ontario, Canada. She graduated college as a graphic artist but has always loved writing. She has written poetry for many years as a means of personal therapy and journaling, both her inner and spiritual growth and day to day events that sparked creativity. She has finally, after several decades released her compilation of poems in hopes it will help heal some that are broken by giving them encouragement, help guide those on a spiritual journey by lending them light and show others that all is possible regardless of the past pains and challenges. And to finally let friends and family truly know her.

*"I hope you enjoy and if even one poem touches you ...
Then my work has been worthwhile."*

Celeste Quackenbush

www.ingramcontent.com/pod-product-compliance
Lightning Source LLC
Chambersburg PA
CBHW071619030726
47598CB00001B/339